Critical Acclaim for Randall Robinson and *The Debt* . . .

"Randall Robinson is the greatest pro-Africa freedom fighter of his generation in America."
—Cornel West, Harvard University professor and author of *Race Matters*

"Randall Robinson is an authentic American hero and a true patriot. He loves his country but is unafraid to rebuke or expose its sins. America is indebted to her black people, and Randall makes the case for why we must not and cannot accept a check marked 'insufficient funds.' "
—Tavis Smiley, author, and host of *BET Tonight*

"Compelling . . . Offers much needed context and rationale for pursuing this critical debate."
—*Detroit Free Press*

"Robinson does it again with this follow-up to his amazing memoir, *Defending the Spirit*. He tells it like it is, and we are all the better—and stronger—for it."
—Edwidge Danticat, author of *The Farming of Bones*

"Provocative . . . Lays out the logic behind reparations and addresses the issue from an economic standpoint."
—*Chicago Sun-Times*

RANDALL ROBINSON, a graduate of Virginia Union University and Harvard Law School, is founder and president of Trans-Africa, the organization that has spearheaded the movement to influence U.S. policies toward Africa and the Caribbean. He played a significant role in the dismantling of apartheid and the restoration of democracy in Haiti. Robinson is the author of *Defending the Spirit* (available from Plume). He lives in Washington, D.C.

THE
DEBT

WHAT AMERICA OWES TO BLACKS

RANDALL ROBINSON

Ⓟ

A PLUME BOOK

PLUME
Published by the Penguin Group
Penguin Putnam Inc., 375 Hudson Street, New York, New York 10014, U.S.A.
Penguin Books Ltd, 27 Wrights Lane, London W8 5TZ, England
Penguin Books Australia Ltd, Ringwood, Victoria, Australia
Penguin Books Canada Ltd, 10 Alcorn Avenue,
Toronto, Ontario, Canada M4V 3B2
Penguin Books (N.Z.) Ltd, 182–190 Wairau Road, Auckland 10, New Zealand

Penguin Books Ltd, Registered Offices:
Harmondsworth, Middlesex, England

Published by Plume, a member of Penguin Putnam Inc.
Previously published in a Dutton edition.

First Plume Printing, January 2001
10 9 8 7 6 5 4 3 2 1

Grateful acknowledgment is made for permission to reprint "We Real Cool"
from *Blacks* by Gwendolyn Brooks. Copyright 1987 by Gwendolyn Brooks.
Reprinted by permission of Third World Press, Inc., Chicago, Illinois.

Ⓟ REGISTERED TRADEMARK—MARCA REGISTRADA

The Library of Congress has catalogued the Dutton edition as follows:
Robinson, Randall
The debt : what America owes to Blacks / Randall Robinson.
p.   cm.
Includes bibliographical references and index.
ISBN 0-525-94524-5 (hc.)
0-452-28210-1 (pbk.)
1. United States—Race relations.   2. Afro-Americans—Civil rights.
3. Afro-Americans—Social conditions.   4. Afro-Americans—Claims.
5. Africa—Civilization—History.   6. Robinson, Randall—Anecdotes.
I. Title.
E185.615.R525 2000
305.8'00973 21—dc21   99-045728

Printed in the United States of America
Original hardcover design by Eve L. Kirch

BOOKS ARE AVAILABLE AT QUANTITY DISCOUNTS WHEN USED TO PROMOTE
PRODUCTS OR SERVICES. FOR INFORMATION PLEASE WRITE TO
PREMIUM MARKETING DIVISION, PENGUIN PUTNAM INC., 375 HUDSON STREET,
NEW YORK, NEW YORK 10014.

For Hazel

CONTENTS

ACKNOWLEDGMENTS

I owe a debt of gratitude to many whose contributions enhanced this work. I begin by thanking professors of law Ibrahim Gassama of the University of Oregon Law School and Robert Westley of Tulane Law School. Their provision of insight, analysis, and legal precedents for reparations proved invaluable to me. Ron Walters of the University of Maryland contributed similarly to my understanding of the national public policy obstacles that African Americans continue to face. In much the same vein, Norman Francis, president of Xavier University, helped me form a picture of the role of academia in America's age-old racial dilemma.

Mwiza Munthali, information specialist for TransAfrica Forum, assisted me with much of the research for this project. Marie Brown, my literary agent, made the project possible as a publishable work. The writer Tonya Bolden read the manuscript and improved it with her thoughtful suggestions. I am thankful to Jennifer Moore and Ann Marlowe for their meticulous editing. I am grateful as well to Monica Duncan, who typed the manuscript.

ACKNOWLEDGMENTS

Last, this work could not have been conceived, begun, or completed without the input of Hazel Ross-Robinson, my wife, friend, and alter ego. She read the manuscript before anyone else. Her insights helped to shape the thoughts to which others would later respond and contribute.

INTRODUCTION

I LOOKED straight up and immediately saw the callous irony, wondering if the slaves who had helped to erect the structure might have bristled at it as quickly as I. The monumental fresco covering 4,664 square feet had been painted by Constantino Brumidi in 1864, just as the hideous 246-year-old American institution of slavery was drawing to a close. According to the United States Capitol Historical Society, Brumidi's *Apotheosis of George Washington* had been painted in the eye of the Rotunda's dome to glorify "the character of George Washington and the principles upon which the United States was founded."

Symbolizing the carapace of American liberty, sixty-odd robed figures are arranged in heroic attitudes around a majestic Washington, before whom a white banner is unfurled bearing the Latin phrase *E Pluribus Unum,* or *one out of many.*

But all of the *many* in the fresco are white.

Beneath the eye and around the rim of the Capitol dome stretches a gray frieze depicting in sequenced scenes America's history from the years of early exploration to the dawn of aviation.

The frieze figures are not all white. Native Americans appear in several of the scenes. In one, the only depiction of an act of violence, a Native American holds back the arms and head of another Native American, as still another Native American coils to bludgeon the pinioned figure. Hmmm.

Although the practice of slavery lay heavily athwart the new country for most of the depicted age, the frieze presents nothing at all from this long, scarring period. No Douglass. No Tubman. No slavery. No blacks, period.

At ground level, set back into the circular stone wall are several huge oil paintings. We see the explorer de Soto discovering the Mississippi River. Next, an elaborately gowned, kneeling Pocahontas receives the baptismal sacrament amidst English gentry in a soaring sanctuary. And there is Columbus triumphantly landing in the Americas.

No reference is made to blacks or slavery in any of the paintings. In the whole of the Rotunda, only a small bust of Martin Luther King Jr. intrudes on an overall iconography of an America that is self-consciously homogeneous and pleased with itself. The King bust is a poor likeness of the man. Its aspect is forlorn. The shoulders sag. The head is bowed, implying surrender, not prayer. The eyes look into the floor, as if the figure understands but cannot quite bear what is going on around it in the Rotunda. A nearby statue of a standing, upward-gazing Thomas Jefferson serves to underscore the King figure's meekness. It was Jefferson who gave to a friend the contract to build the Capitol. The tall statue's countenance is proprietary, of the Rotunda if not of the country.

After completing the fresco in the eye of the dome, Brumidi spent many years painting frescoes and oils for the interior of the Capitol. In his words, he wanted to "beautify the Capitol of the one country in which there is liberty."

The frescoes, the friezes, the oil paintings, the composite art of the Rotunda—this was to be America's iconographic idea of itself. On proud display for the world's regard, the pictorial symbols of American democracy set forth our core social attitudes about democracy's subtenets: fairness, inclusiveness, openness, tolerance, and, in the broadest sense, freedom.

To erect the building that would house the art that symbolized American democracy, the United States government sent out a request for one hundred slaves. The first stage of the Capitol's construction would run from 1793 to 1802. In exchange for the slaves' labor the government agreed to pay their *owners* five dollars per month per slave.

Slaves were not only made to labor on the Capitol building but also to do much of the work in implementing Pierre-Charles L'Enfant's grand design for the whole of the District of Columbia. L'Enfant had decided to place the Capitol building on Jenkins Hill and the President's Palace (later the White House) on another hill, which was at the time covered by an orchard. Slaves were used to clear a broad swath of forest between the sites for the two buildings.

I looked up again at Brumidi's celebration of the "principles upon which the United States was founded" and visualized the glistening backs of blacks with ropes and pulleys heaving the ponderous stones of the dome into place. I then went down a floor to a gift kiosk run by the Capitol Historical Society to look for books about the Capitol's construction. I found two: *In the Greatest Solemn Dignity* and *Uncle Sam's Architect: Builders of the Capitol*. Neither book mentioned anything about the use of slave labor.

I returned to the Rotunda and took a seat on one of the low-backed cushioned benches arranged around the curved wall of the large room. I took out the notes I had made from a telephone discussion with William Allen of the Architect of the Capitol office. Allen had said that arkose sandstone blocks—in all likelihood the ones into which the huge and heroic oil paintings are set—were brought by slaves and oxen from the Aquia Creek quarry in Stafford County, Virginia. They had been mined and loaded onto boats by slaves and brought forty miles up the Potomac River before being unloaded near the old Navy Yard, which is very close to TransAfrica's former office on Eighth Street S.E. On the construction site, stone blocks that could not be handled by oxen were handled by slaves and pulleys.

My reverie was interrupted by a group of Asian tourists who stepped in front of me to peer up into the dome. (They credit America as America credits itself.) The worn and pitted stones on which the tourists stood had doubtless been hauled into position by slaves, for whom the most arduous of tasks were reserved. They had fired and stacked the bricks. They had mixed the mortar. They had sawn the long timbers in hellishly dangerous pits with one slave out of the pit and another in, often nearly buried alive in sawdust.

The third phase of the Capitol construction (the second occurred after 1812) would take place during the Civil War, just as Brumidi set about to paint the first of his "liberty" frescoes for the building. During the war, slaves dislocated in the turmoil gravitated to Union soldiers, who often brought them to Washington to be put to work on the Capitol. William Allen called them "spoils of war" and "contraband slaves." When I asked him about the term "contraband slave," he grew quiet as if questioning for the first time the purpose of my general inquiry about the use of black slave labor.

Atop the dome of the Capitol stands the *Statue of Freedom* in the figure of a Native American female warrior clad in a star-festooned helmet and flowing robes. The statue was designed for $3,000 by Thomas Crawford in Rome, Italy, in 1856. In 1863, it was cast in bronze in Bladensburg, Maryland, at a foundry owned by Clark Mills, whom the government paid $23,736 for his work.

Philip Reed, a slave owned by Mills, was given the responsibility for casting the *Statue of Freedom* and loading its five sections, each weighing more than a ton, onto reinforced wagons for the slow trip to the east grounds of the Capitol. There, Reed and other slaves reassembled *Freedom* to make certain that all of its pieces would fit together. The task of assembling *Freedom* took thirty-one days. The statue was then disassembled, hoisted, and reassembled by slaves on the *tholos*, a pedestal on the dome surmounted by a globe.

I sat on the bench musing for a good while. I love buildings. My earliest ambition was to be an architect, driven perhaps by a child's yearning for immortality. Buildings are in some respects like people. They run the gamut from hideous to beautiful. Some are powerful. Some are weak. Most are terribly ordinary. A few are works of surpassing genius. Virtually all provoke emotional reaction: awe, inadequacy, lightheartedness, revulsion, exaltation, boredom.

Buildings are like people in other ways as well. They are usually successful at revealing only what they wish the viewer to see. They embody human characteristics. They have souls, memories, traditions, and larger meanings that sum up to well more than the inert materials that constitute them. They clothe themselves in veneers of deceitful finery. They cornice. They gild. They dazzle. They inspire. They lie. And they keep their secrets very well. *Beneath* the grandeur, I thought as my eyes were drawn back up into the dome.

A full half of the people on the floor were looking up with me. Most of them were white Americans. At least a fourth of them, though, were tourists who appeared to be from either India or Pakistan, from Japan perhaps, and from western Europe. These upturned faces, bathed by the sun's rays streaming through the clerestory windows in the dome's hatband, looked to be in worship, transfixed.

I could not completely place myself outside this spell. Everything about the room was dwarfing—the scale of the art, the size of the round chamber, the height and sheer majesty of the dome. It had all combined to achieve the Founding Fathers' objective, which was, I am certain, to awe. And to hide the building's and America's secrets.

I thought, then, what a fitting metaphor the Capitol Rotunda was for America's racial sorrows. In the magnificence of its boast, in the tragedy of its truth, in the effrontery of its deceit.

This was the house of Liberty, and it had been built by slaves. Their backs had ached under its massive stones. Their lungs had clogged with its mortar dust. Their bodies had wilted under its heavy load-bearing timbers. They had been paid only in the coin of pain. Slavery lay across American history like a monstrous cleaving sword, but the Capitol of the United States steadfastly refused to divulge its complicity, or even slavery's very occurrence. It gave full lie to its own gold-spun half-truth.

It shrank from the simplest honesty. It mocked the shining eyes of the innocent. It kept from us all—black, brown, white—the chance to begin again as co-owners of a national democratic idea. It blinded us all to our past and, with the same stroke, to any common future.

At the dawn of the twenty-first century African Americans lag the American mainstream in virtually every area of statistical measure. Neither blacks nor whites know accurately why. The answer can be found only in the distant past, a past as deliberately obscured as the Capitol's secrets.

Solutions to our racial problems are possible, but only if our society can be brought to face up to the massive crime of slavery and all that it has wrought.

Now never begins yesterday. To set afoot a new and whole black woman and man, we must first tell the victims what happened to them—before and after America was new.

Insights crystallize often under the oddest circumstances. Like a melodic idea to a composer, a light pops on for no apparent reason, allowing understanding where one has been well trained not to have it. In a small village in western Turkey a while back, I watched a dervish whirl in his mesmerizing dance, performing a ritual a thousand years old. I have witnessed such time-honored practices in forty-five countries across the world. Seeing disparate peoples in far-flung cultures held safely above the abyss by the stout rope of their traditions, I have always been left, as I keenly was in the case of the whirling dervish, with a feeling of sweet sadness, perhaps envy even. For the armaments of culture and history that have protected the tender interiors of peoples from the dawn of time have been premeditatedly stripped from the black victims of American slavery.

No race, no ethnic or religious group, has suffered so much over so long a span as blacks have, and do still, at the hands of those who benefited, with the connivance of the United States government, from slavery and the century of legalized American racial hostility that followed it. It is a miracle that the victims—weary dark souls long shorn of a venerable and ancient identity—have survived at all, stymied as they are by the blocked roads to economic equality.

This book is about the great still-unfolding massive crime of official and unofficial America against Africa, African slaves, and their descendants in America.

I do not honor here with much attention the diversionary noises between protagonists and antagonists over notions of affirmative action. For while I support affirmative action, I believe that those who would camp blacks in an exitless corner expending all energy defending its thin dime do the black community no service.

It is, again, not that affirmative action concepts are wrong-headed. They indeed are not. They should remain in place. But such programs are not *solutions* to our problems. They are palliatives that help people like *me*, who are poised to succeed when given half a chance. They do little for the millions of African Americans bottom-mired in urban hells by the savage time-release social debilitations of American slavery. They do little for those Americans, disproportionately black, who inherit grinding poverty, poor nutrition, bad schools, unsafe neighborhoods, low expectation, and overburdened mothers. Lamentably, there will always be poverty. But African Americans are overrepresented in that economic class for one reason and one reason only: American slavery and the vicious climate that followed it. Affirmative action, should it survive, will never come anywhere near to balancing the books here. While I can speak only for myself, I choose not to spend my limited gifts and energy and time fighting *only* for the penny due when a fortune is owed.

At long last, let America contemplate the scope of its enduring human-rights wrong against the whole of a people. Let the vision of blacks not become so blighted from a sunless eternity that we fail to *see* the staggering breadth of America's crime against us.

Solutions must be tailored to the scope of the crime in a way that would make the victim whole. In this case, the psychic and economic injury is enormous, multidimensional and long-running. Thus must be America's restitution to blacks for the damage done.

As Germany and other interests that profited *owed* reparations to Jews following the holocaust of Nazi persecution, America and other interests that profited *owe* reparations to blacks following the holocaust of African slavery which has carried forward from slavery's inception for 350-odd years to the end of U.S. government–embraced racial discrimination—an end that arrived, it would seem, only just yesterday.

For centuries blacks have fought their battles an episode at a time, losing sight of the full ugly picture. Seeing it whole all but defies description.

I have tried in these pages to sketch the outlines of a story that stretches from the dawn of civilization to the present. The dilemma of blacks in the world cannot possibly be understood without taking the long view of history. I have, by necessity, painted basic themes with a broad brush and make no claim to comprehensiveness. (For those with an appetite for more information, a resource list follows the text.) Here my intent is to stimulate, not to sate. To pose the question, to invite the debate. To cause America to compensate, after three and a half centuries, for a long-avoided wrong.

1

RECLAIMING OUR ANCIENT SELF

When I discover who I am, I'll be free.
—Ralph Ellison

I WAS BORN in 1941, but my black soul is much older than that. Its earliest incarnations occurred eons ago on another continent somewhere in the mists of prehistory. Thus, there are two selves: one born a mere fifty-eight years ago; the other, immortal, who has lost sight of the trail of his long story. I am this new self and an ancient self. I need both to be whole. Yet there is a war within, and I feel a great wanting of the spirit.

The immortal self—the son of the shining but distant African ages—tells the embattled, beleaguered, damaged self, the

> *It is at Heliopolis that the most learned of the Egyptian antiquaries are said to be found. . . . As to practical matters, they are all agreed in saying that the Egyptians by their study of astronomy discovered the solar year and were the first to divide it into twelve parts. . . . They also told me that the Egyptians first brought into use the names of the twelve gods, which the Greeks took over from them, and were the first to assign altars and images and temples to the gods, and to carve figures in stone.*
>
> —Herodotus (circa 450 B.C.)

modern self, what he needs to remember of his ancient traditions. But the modern self simply cannot remember and thus cannot believe. The modern self has desperately tried, but the effort has been only marginally fruitful. Maliciously shorn of his natural identity for so long, he can too easily get lost in another's.

In any case, in America, there is little space for *before*.

Before the Mayflower . . .

Before that Dutch man-o'-war docked at Jamestown Landing in August 1619 with twenty Africans in its belly . . .

Before the Middle Passage . . .

And when *before* is on view, invariably it is white. Sight lines to the *before* that I require, that I crave, are blocked.

———

From the times of ancient scribes, history has been written and studied, traditions honored, gods worshiped, monuments to the greater glory erected, institutions sustained in countless

> *They [i.e., the Greek historians relied upon by the writer] say also that the Egyptians are colonists sent out by the Ethiopians [i.e., not the modern Ethiopians, but, the black peoples from inner Africa south of Egypt], Osiris having been the leader of the colony. For speaking generally, what is now Egypt, they maintain, was not land but sea when in the beginning the universe was being formed; afterwards, however, as the Nile during the times of its inundating carried down the mud from [the land of the black peoples], land was gradually built up from the deposit. . . . And the larger part of the customs of the Egyptians are, they [i.e., the Greek historians] hold, Ethiopian, the colonists still preserving their ancient manners.*
>
> —Diodorus Siculus (circa 50 B.C.)

cultures coursing humanity's mosaic of peoples across the millennia like life-giving rivers. These are not extraneous behaviors. They are essential to the health of any people's spirit. They are givers of collective self-worth, cheaters of mortality, binding frail short lives into a people's ongoing, epic cumulative achievement.

> *We spent the night on the island [of Mombasa] and then set sail for Kilwa, the principal town on the [East African] coast, the greater part of whose inhabitants are Zanj of very black complexion. . . . A merchant told me that Sofala is half a month's march from Kilwa, and that between Sofala and Yufi in the country of the Limiin is a month's march. Powdered gold is brought from Yufi to Sofala. . . .*
>
> *Kilwa is one of the most beautiful and well-constructed towns in the world. The whole of it is elegantly built.*
>
> —Ibn Battuta (1331)

Though it would appear that Americans grow less knowledgeable by the day, there are still many American schoolchildren who recognize the Roman Colosseum, the Great Wall of China, the Parthenon, the Tower of London. From Africa, only the great pyramids of Egypt enjoy such broad recognition, and they are popularly and wrongly attributed to a civilization not spawned from Africa's interior. By and large, only behind the most obscure doors of high academe can one unearth a mention of the great African empires and polities of antiquity like Kush, Benin, Meroe, Djenne, Ghana, and Songhay. Few Americans, if shown photographs of the stone walls of Monomatapa or the magnificent ruins at Axum, would be able to identify these ancient African survivals.

Far too many Americans of African descent believe their history starts in America with bondage and struggles forward from there toward today's second-class citizenship. The cost of this obstructed view of ourselves, of our history, is incalculable. How can we be *collectively* successful if we have no idea or, worse, the wrong idea of who we were and, therefore, are? We are history's amnesiacs fitted with the memories of others. Our minds can be trained for individual career success but our group morale, the very soul of us, has been devastated by the assumption that what has not been told to us about ourselves does not exist to be told.

Previous European scholarship knew that the foundations of European civilization derived from classical Greek civilization. That scholarship further accepted what the Greeks had laid down as patently obvious: that classical Greek civilization derived in its religion, its philosophy, its mathematics and much else, from the ancient civilizations of Africa above all from Egypt of the Pharaohs. To those 'founding fathers' in classical Greece, any notion that Africans were inferior, morally or intellectually, would have seemed silly. —Basil Davidson, *Africa in History* (1991)

This then is the nub of it. America's contemporary racial problems cannot be solved, racism cannot be arrested, achievement gaps cannot be fully closed until Americans—*all Americans*—are repaired in their views of Africa's role in history.

Like it or not, the races are fixed in their views of each other. While restrained by the diaphanous fetters of polite hypocrisy, most in the world, including Africa and her progeny, perceive

Africa and blacks generally to be lagging the field in achievement. This was not always the case, and has only *been* the case for the merest moment in the long march of human progress. To be made large and formidable and masterful again—to be whole again—blacks need to know the land of their forebears when its civilizations were verifiably equal to any in the world.

Blacks, and no less whites, need to know that in the centuries preceding the Atlantic slave trade and the invention of a virulent racism to justify it, the idea of black inferiority did not exist.

> *I say with the fullest confidence that you could strike out every single reference to [Othello's] black skin and the play would be essentially the same. Othello's trouble is that he is an outsider. He is not a Venetian. He is a military bureaucrat, a technician, hired to fight for Venice, a foreign country. The Senate has no consciousness whatever of his color. That is a startling fact but true. They haven't to make allowances for it. It simply has no place in their minds.* —C. L. R. James

William Shakespeare wrote *Othello* between 1602 and 1604. Had Shakespeare lived and written in the eighteenth century, *Othello* would never have had a Moor as the protagonist. The sea change in global racial perceptions, principally occasioned by the Atlantic slave trade and its justifiers, was that pervasive.

In the modern social context of spoken and unspoken assumptions about race, the apparent nonexistence of race as a basis for prejudgment during the early and middle ages may strain credulity for many. As does the truth of individual black achievement and prominence in the far past.

Take, for instance, an edition of the CBS News program *60 Minutes* that aired September 20, 1998. A segment of the program focused on who might succeed Pope John Paul II as head of the Roman Catholic Church. Cardinal Francis Arinze, a Nigerian, was described as having a reasonable chance of becoming the next pope.

Would Catholics bolt the church *en masse* if the College of Cardinals were to select Cardinal Arinze as the next pope? Could the church politically afford to name an African pope? Catholic hierarchs and historians reviewed four centuries of Vatican history and puzzled with CBS's Morley Safer over such questions and the chances for a revolutionary breakthrough. The discussion had a milestone-aborning feel to it. But, oh, how misleading this was.

Never once was it mentioned that in the first millennium the Catholic Church had three popes who were either from Africa or of African descent; Saint Victor I (189–99), Saint Miltiades (311–14), and Saint Gelasius I (492–96) of whom, in his 1996 book *Popes through the Ages*, James Brusher wrote, "Although a great writer, Gelasius made his strongest impression as a man of holiness. . . . He was outstanding for his sense of justice and above all for his charity to the poor." Born in Rome, but described in the *Oxford Dictionary of Popes* to have been of African descent and in P. G. Maxwell-Stuart's *Chronicle of the Popes* as African by nationality, Gelasius was remembered as "great even among the saints." Much is written in the literature of the episcopates of these three African popes, but nothing that would suggest controversy about their ethnic identity. The three popes were selected, they served with distinction, and that was that. Such would be hard to imagine in today's climate.

Was *60 Minutes*'s omission of Saints Victor, Miltiades, and

Gelasius an oversight? Certainly, in preparing for the segment, the *60 Minutes* researchers must have come upon the early african popes. What were the researchers thinking?

Giving them the benefit of the doubt, they had either: (1) looked directly upon, but not seen, the voluminous references in the early church texts; (2) misread the early church texts; or (3) elected not to believe the early church texts.

————————

As I write this, I picture my immortal soul in the body of a man in the year 1831 A.D. living out my time in West Africa. I am eighty years old by then. I grow poorer by the day and wish to die before my resources are fully depleted. The physical decline of my village parallels the long, slow decline of my material living conditions. I am weak, but that is to be expected at my age. I am more troubled by the ineffable and unascribable sadness that I suffer of late. I sometimes cry for no reason. My kinspeople are mystified and saddened for me. Our family compound is deteriorated but commodious. It mirrors the problems of our troubled land.

Great age affords me a long view of past events. It is that view that fills me with pride. The view's dimming light, I believe, may be one source of this unshakable disconsolacy as well.

In the 1750s my grandparents filled my small child's head with stories about our people when we were a great power in the world. My grandfather was a much respected scholar who knew the stories of ancient empire well and told them to my siblings and me more out of duty than pleasure. He knew things that few others knew, sometimes things that had happened long ago and beyond the great sea. I cannot remember the stories so well anymore and that too saddens me. I think that I am failing our young, who will have no memory of our greatness if I can no longer recall the far past for them.

Was Meroe the place of the sumptuous stone buildings? I think but I'm not sure anymore.

There are times, though increasingly further apart, when my memory works as it once did, when I can remember well Grandfather's stories and the rigorous studies of my youth under his tutelage. Grandfather had read all the works of the ancient scholars. The scholars whose writings I could not read for myself, Grandfather told me about. Many who wrote about my region were from faraway places, like al-Bakri of Cordoba who had, seven hundred years before, chronicled the empire of Ghana. Mahmud Kati and Abd al-Rahman were scholars who were born in this region and lived in nearby Timbuktu. They too had written much about the great kingdom of Ghana, which had been succeeded in wealth and power by my own Mali, which in turn had given way to the even more powerful empire of Songhay. My country and Songhay together were as large, I had learned, as the whole of western Europe. Ibn Battuta, the Moroccan scholar who had traversed Africa and visited Turkey and traveled as far east as China, wrote of us in the year 1352: "One of the good features [of the government and people of Mali] is their lack of oppression. They are the farthest removed from it. Another of their good features is the security which embraces the whole country. Neither the traveler nor the man who stays at home has anything to fear from thief or from usurper."

The Mandinka people, to which I belong, formed the core of our empire. The greatest of our emperors was Mansa Musa who rose to power in 1312 and died in 1337. It was under him that the cities of Timbuktu and Djenne launched their long eras of scholarship and learning, with notice of the excellence of their schools of law and theology reaching far into Muslim Asia.

The emperor erected great mosques of brick, expanded the military, and built a trade network so vast that in 1375, thirty-eight years after his death, the Majorcan cartographer Cresques depicted traders from all of North Africa marching to our markets. The Muslim dinar, the gold coin that had supplanted the *denarius aureus* of Byzantium as the most respected standard of value in much of the world, was minted from our region's gold, Asia Minor's sources having long since been exhausted.

In those times, our empires were world powers. It was our gold that undergirded the world trading system. Europe was only just emerging from the poverty and chaos that followed the collapse of the Western Roman Empire. Their new money would be based on our gold. No other sources existed anywhere.

I knew less about the coastal people who lived to the unfathomable east, beyond the great lake, along the littoral of the *Sea of the Zanj* (sea of the black people), as the Arab writers called it. But Grandfather had read of them in a very old book that he prized more than any other single thing he owned. As its parchment was powdery and fragile, I was allowed to read the book only in his presence. It had been written in 925 A.D. by Abu al-Hasan al-Masudi. I remember that the name of the book was *The Meadows of Gold and Mines of Gems*. It told of the kingdom of the Zanj and a leader who bore the title of *waqlimi*, which means "supreme lord." The Zanj, al-Masudi wrote, "give this title to their sovereign because he has been chosen to govern them with equity. But once he becomes tyrannical and departs from the rules of justice, they cause him to die and exclude his posterity from succession to the throne, for they claim that in behaving thus he ceases to be the son of the Master, that is the king of heaven and earth."

Grandfather said that in the year 1414 the leader of Malindi along the same coast to the east made a gift of a giraffe to China. The Chinese emperor, having never seen one, had thought the giraffe to be a mythical creature and demonstrated his appreciation by sending an ocean-sailing ship that bore away to China Malindi's ambassador to be thanked personally by the emperor in the year 1417. The ship had been under the command of an Admiral Cheng-Ho. Grandfather showed this reference to me in another of his countless books.

Not long after this, the sun went out across the whole of our land. For it was around the year 1500 that the Portuguese arrived along the coast to the east. They seemed a curious people, simultaneously looting and admiring. One of their chroniclers, a Duarte Barbosa, wrote of the coastal city-state of Kilwa that it "has many handsome houses of stone and mortar, with many windows such as our own houses have, and very well arranged streets." Of Mombasa, further north along the coast, Barbosa had described "a very handsome place with tall stone and mortar houses well aligned in streets as they are in Kilwa, as well as being a place of much traffic with a good harbor where are always moored boats of many kinds, and also great ships." It is strange, I think, that this Barbosa man would write such things about *buildings* while, not three score years before his account, his people, the Portuguese, had begun stealing our people.

You might have thought that today had been a good day for

. . . our men had very great toil in the capture of those who were swimming, for they dived like CORMORANTS, so that they could not get hold of them, and the capture of the second man caused them to lose all the others. For he was so valiant that two men, strong as they were, could not drag him into the boat until they took a boathook and caught him above one eye, and the pain of this made him abate his courage, and allow himself to be put inside the boat. —Gomes Eannes de Zurara, *Chronicle of the Discovery and Conquest of Guinea*, 1444

me, inasmuch as my mind has been clear. But such days, mercifully rare, leave me more, rather than less, depressed.

For the whole of my life and a time before, many of those I have known, including my sister and two brothers, have been captured and (I later learned) boarded on ships at the coast. My family did not know where the ships went and never heard word about my sister and brothers again.

Are they alive somewhere and old like me? I wish I could know only that. I am crying again. This practice of stealing our people continues to this day. Our young people cannot sit still to listen to tales of glory from a dying old man while they fear being stolen.

Grandfather had hoped that those who had been captured would, as is the custom here, be set free or become a member of the new tribe. But none who had been taken away were ever seen again.

I am old and broken now and I cry. I cry for all who have been abducted, for this empty broken land, for Grandfather's stories that are fading in my memory, for the souls of my ancestors who gave art and craft and science to the whole of the world.

The American writer Thomas Paine would likely have sympathized with my imagined Malian soul-sharer and his scholarly eighteenth-century grandfather. Before slavery, Paine had seen Africa as a fertile land of industrious, quiet-living, peace-loving people. On March 8, 1775, Paine, soon to be one of the leaders of the American Revolution, published "African Slavery in America" in the *Pennsylvania Journal and Weekly Advertiser*. He wrote:

> That some desperate wretches should be willing to steal and enslave men by violence and murder for gain is rather lamentable than strange. . . . The managers of that trade themselves, and others, testify that many of these African nations inhabit fertile countries, are industrious farmers, enjoy plenty and lived quietly, averse to war, before the Europeans debauched them with liquors, and bribed them against one another, and that these inoffensive people are brought into slavery, by stealing them, tempting kings to sell subjects, which they have no right to do, and hiring one tribe to war against another to catch prisoners. By such wicked and inhuman ways the English are said to enslave toward one hundred thousand yearly; of which thirty thousand are supposed to die by barbarous treatment in the first year; besides all that are slain in the unnatural wars excited to take them. So much innocent blood have the managers and supporters of this inhuman trade to answer for to the common Lord of all.

In 1434, when the Portuguese approached the land mass of Africa, they were to discover in the regions south of the Sahara peoples who had long since developed complex economic, political, and social systems. Cities along the Niger River, such as Segu, Kankan, Timbuktu, Djenne, and Gao, ranged from ten to thirty thousand people. Katsina and Kano, Hausa cities, had each as many as a hundred thousand inhabitants. Iron and steel of high quality were smelted. Copper was a fruit of local industry. Knives, spears, axes, and hoes were produced by Africans for African households. Such was the quality of goldsmithery that a Dutch captain would write: "The thread and texture of their hatbands and chaining is so fine that . . . our ablest European artists would find it difficult to imitate them." Africans had made finely decorated pottery for centuries. They wove, wore, and traded linen and cotton.

All of this—centuries of economic and social development— was about to change.

On August 8, 1444, six hundred-ton caravels made port in the Algarve region of Portugal and unloaded a cargo of 235 African slaves, who were displayed in an open field. The Portuguese chronicler Gomes Eannes de Zurara was to describe the scene: "What heart could be so hard as not to be pierced with piteous feeling to see that company? For some kept their heads low, and their faces bathed in tears, looking one upon another. Others stood groaning very dolorously, looking up to the height of heaven, fixing their eyes upon it, crying out loudly, as if asking help from the Father of Nature; others struck their faces with the palms of their hands, throwing themselves at full length upon the ground; while others made lamentations in the manner of a dirge, after the custom of their country."

By 1448 the Portuguese had carried off a thousand Africans. The number would grow exponentially over the next century.

King Affonso of Kongo (Congo) wrote to King João of Portugal in 1526: "Each day the traders are kidnapping our people—children of this country, sons of our nobles and vassals, even people of our own family. [King Affonso's nephews and grandchildren had been kidnapped while en route to Portugal for religious education and sent into slavery in Brazil.] . . . This corruption and depravity are so widespread that our land is entirely depopulated. . . . It is our wish that this Kingdom not be a place for the trade or transport of slaves."

King João wrote back: "You . . . tell me that you want no slave-trading in your domains, because this trade is depopulating your country. . . . The Portuguese there, on the contrary, tell me how vast the Congo is, and how it is so thickly populated that it seems as if no slave has ever left."

While King Affonso was no stranger to slavery, which was practiced throughout most of the known world, he had understood slavery as a condition befalling prisoners of war, criminals, and debtors, out of which slaves could earn, or even marry, their way. This was nothing like seeing this wholly new and brutal commercial practice of slavery where tens of thousands of his subjects were dragged off in chains. When the king sent emissaries on a long and arduous sea voyage to appeal to the pope in Rome, the emissaries were arrested upon their arrival in Lisbon.

By 1831 the Africans who had been sold into slavery numbered in the millions. America, along with Europe, had fallen in behind a leading German thinker, Georg Hegel, in justifying slavery to itself and to the world. Declared Hegel:

The Negro exhibits the natural man in his completely wild and untamed state. We must lay aside all thought of reverence and morality—all that we call feeling—if we could rightly comprehend him: there is nothing harmonious with humanity to be found in his type of character. . . . [Africa] is no historical part of the world; it has no movement or development to show.

Africans would henceforth be seen as without worth or history.

Darkness. Opaque, impenetrable darkness. Africa's past before the slave trade, quite literally, had disappeared. And that continent's chattel issue, for a limitless future the world around, would become history's orphans. Languages, customs, traditions, rituals, faiths, mores, taboos—all vitals of the immortal larger self—gone, extinguished. A seeming eternal identity, a people's whole memory, crushed under the remorseless commerce of slavery.

No people can live successfully, fruitfully, triumphantly without strong memory of their past, without reading the future within the context of some reassuring past, without implanting reminders of that past in the present. Consider the following passage from David S. Ariel's 1995 book *What Do Jews Believe?*:

Each generation retells the sacred myths of the Jewish people. In each telling of the story, we relate to the narratives told by previous generations while modifying and changing them. For example, the sacred myth of the Exodus from Egypt became the basis of the Passover Seder and the Haggadah, the written account of the Exodus. Each Passover, the story of how God freed the ancient Israelites from Egypt in order to give them the Torah is retold.

> *There are in Timbuktu numerous judges, doctors [of letters] and priests [i.e., learned Muslims]. [The ruler] greatly honors scholarship. Here too they sell many handwritten books that arrive from Barbary [i.e., North Africa]. More profit is had from their sale than from any other merchandise.* —Leo Africanus (1550)

Jews, Arabs, Turks, Russians, Finns, Swedes, Czechs, Uzbeks, Macedonians, Estonians, Malayans, Cathayans, Japanese, Sinhalese—one and all planetwide—have a nurturing access to the fullness of their myriad histories, histories that often seem as old as time.

African Americans must spiritually survive from the meager basket of a few mean yesterdays. No chance for significant group progress there. None. For we have been largely overwhelmed by a majority culture that wronged us dramatically, emptied our memories, undermined our self-esteem, implanted us with palatable voices, and stripped us along the way of the sheerest corona of self-definition. We alone are presumed pastless, left to cobble self-esteem from a vacuum of stolen history.

By default, we must define ourselves by our ongoing tribulations and those who mete them out to us. Otherwise, we have little in the way of a long-held interior idea of who we are.

While I am anything but the passionate conspiracy-phobic, the contemporary social results seem anything but accidental.

2

TAKING ACCOUNT OF THE LONG-TERM PSYCHIC DAMAGE

Every race has a soul, and the soul of that race finds expression in its institutions, and to kill those institutions is to kill the soul. . . . No people can profit or be helped under institutions which are not the outcome of their own character.

—Edward Blyden (1903)

I N THE FALL of 1998 I went to the television studio of the University of the District of Columbia to tape an interview about my memoir, *Defending the Spirit*. Before the taping, Ed Jones, the station's general manager and an old friend, introduced me to a twelve-year-old neighborhood black boy who was there with his mentor, a student at the college, to hear my discussion. Billy was an attractive and pleasant boy with a stocky build and intelligent eyes.

"Billy," said Ed, "have you ever heard of Randall Robinson?"

"No."

Jesus, Ed, you might have spared me the sure-fire blow to the egoplexus.

"Well, Mr. Robinson is the president of TransAfrica. You've heard of TransAfrica, right?"

Christ almighty, Ed.

"No."

"Well, Mr. Robinson led the effort in the United States to free Nelson Mandela in South Africa. You've heard of Nelson Mandela, right?"

Now here we go.

"No."

On my way home from meeting Billy, I visualized the boy on a walk with his mentor on the long grassy Mall in Washington. He is surrounded by monuments and memorials. They can mean little to him although he consciously tries to compensate for his lack of emotional engagement. It isn't that he has no interest. He does. The monuments and buildings are big and impressive. Lincoln, Jefferson, Washington, Roosevelt. Still, he does not feel anything much, other than small. Not small but *small*. The monuments don't seem intended for him. They do seem, from the look on their faces, intended for the white family of four from Nebraska standing near him. Look at them, sunny with pride in their ridiculous plaid vacation wear and dangling Kodaks. Mall-trekking well-scrubbed Norman Rockwell pieces of Americana as remote from Billy as the monuments that captivate them.

Where am I? Who am I? Why am I here?

The questions remain buried and unphrased in Billy's psyche, with only boredom as a sustaining frame for the aimless remarks he makes to his mentor. The monuments, neutral before sighting the Nebraska family, stand now in odd rebuke.

"When are we going home?"

"Soon. But you need to know this stuff. History is important."

"Why?"

The mentor does not answer. Billy is exhausting his script and testing his patience.

"What is that? Over there with the long line?"

"That's the holocaust memorial."

"What's a holocaust?"

"During World War Two, the Germans tried to kill all of the Jews in Europe. Six million Jews died. That memorial helps us remember the terrible thing that happened there."

"Oh yeah?" Genuine curiosity. Approval. "What about us?" Hopeful now.

"What do you mean? What about us?"

———

The estimates vary. Anywhere from ten to twenty-five million Africans died in slave ships en route from Africa to the Americas. A lifetime of bondage awaited those who survived the passage. This massive crime against humanity—the enslavement and exploitation of tens of millions of human beings—is an American holocaust. (The extermination of the Native American population is another.) Yet one can scour the commemorative architecture of the nation's capital and find little evidence that America's racial holocaust ever occurred.

It is as if, since its very establishment, America had chosen to hold, as Napoleon would, that "history is the myth that men choose to believe." The crypto-Machiavellians who serve as the perennial stewards of American public affairs understand that people on the whole are about as malleable as their history can be made to be. The landscape is rife with examples, from historically overarching lies and half-truths to popular culture deceits.

It is well known that Thomas Jefferson had slaves. It is less well known that he had them chased and brought back when they escaped.

Or consider Charles Lindbergh. When the nation needed a hero, Lindbergh flew the Atlantic nonstop from New York to Paris in the spring of 1927. Even in an era of relatively primitive communications technology, few in the world failed to learn almost instantly of Lindbergh's feat. His ensuing hero status has survived for over seventy years largely untarnished, although Lindbergh, a self-described racist, had written in *Reader's Digest* in 1939 that aviation was "a gift from heaven . . . a tool specially shaped for Western hands . . . one of those priceless possessions which permit the white race to live at all in a pressing sea of yellow, black and brown." He urged the U.S. not to war with but to join Germany in forming a "Western Wall of race and arms which can hold back either a Genghis Khan or the infiltration of inferior blood."

In Hollywood, press agents have gone to great lengths to suppress reports that film star Arnold Schwarzenegger's father was a member of the Austrian Nazi party. While the sins of the father should not be visited upon the son, that is not why the flacks are busy. Of course, sanitizing history is hardly a new practice. Socrates advanced ideas for selective breeding to produce a super race. The ideas were later copied by Nazi Germany. Such theories are now seldom associated with Socrates.

In the animated Dreamworks movie *Prince of Egypt* the ancient Egyptians are drawn to appear more Arab than African. But the ancient Egyptians came originally from Africa's interior to the south. They were not Arabs, not people from Arabia, but indigenous Africans. Egyptian civilization was thousands of years old by the time the Arabs, with a modest army under General 'Amr ibn as- 'As, entered in December of 639 A.D.

Back around 3000 B.C. the First Dynasty of the Old Kingdom of Egypt had been founded by one Narmer. A stone likeness of the pharaoh survives, its features offering convincing evidence that the ancient Egyptians who built the great pyramids were black. (Pictures of Narmer's likeness and those of succeeding pharaohs can be found in UNESCO's *General History of Africa*, volume II, pages 52–57. Have a look.)

Three millennia later Egypt's throne had passed to Cleopatra, who herself may have been a good deal darker than any of the actresses who portrayed her on screen. The queen belonged to the Ptolemaic dynasty, a line of Macedonian Greeks who had ruled Egypt since its conquest by Alexander the Great, but the identity of one of her grandmothers is unknown. This grandmother may have been a concubine, not a member of the Ptolemaic family. Cleopatra was the only one of the family to speak the Egyptian language. At least one Roman historian described her as dark-skinned. All this leaves open the question of whether she looked black or white. But it is not likely that she had the alabaster skin or violet eyes of Elizabeth Taylor.

It is even less likely that a Semitic Christ of two thousand years ago even vaguely resembled the ubiquitous blond image most Americans believe to be something near to Christ's actual appearance.

Again, I am not suggesting the presence of any grand conspiracy to suppress or distort history or ephemeral information. Accuracy can be elusive. For more than twenty years I have read newspaper accounts of developments in Africa and the Caribbean in which I have had direct firsthand involvement. Often the coverage has been fraught with factual error, critical omission, and wrongheaded perspective. Most of the misdescription was due, I suppose, to inadvertence or incompetence as opposed to bad intentions. The point is this. Even well-meaning, competent journalists sometime misreport events that occur in the world only days before. Journalism is not an exact science. Historiography is a hundredfold less exact than journalism—even when historians believe themselves sincerely trying to be objective. Their subjects are long dead. Records are incomplete or nonexistent. Flawed premises beget more flawed premises. And then, of course, there are the built-in distortions. Would-be Machiavellis, some long dead before the Florentine statesman himself ever lived, anticipate the historian's enquiries by booby-trapping evidence, laying false trails, and liquidating artifacts. (This might have been what Napoleon had in mind when he blew off the nose of the Sphinx. Or was it Mohammed Sa'im al-Dahr who did it, in 1378 A.D.? No one really knows.)

In his book *Black Spark, White Fire*, historian Richard Poe makes a case that black Egyptians were among the first philosophers and explorers, traveling as far from Egypt as Russia and turning up with the Romans at Troy. Has such knowledge been suppressed heretofore, or simply lost? According to Poe, "History was designed to justify European domination."

None of this begins to adequately explain the near total disappearance of Africa's past and the denial of its information to the modern world. To me. To Billy.

First, though, a small digression—a word about wording.

Social policy advocates are prone to talk one way and write another. They speak with compassion and empathy but write like academic prisoners of statistics and bar charts. We cerebral activists are innocent victims of our very traditional training. Oftener than not, there is no pain or joy, no hope or despair in our writing. Emotion is verboten. Objectivity is the object. We liken its straight lines to high intellect.

Only our speech is personal or sincere. Even in its periodic untruth it requires of us, at the very least, accountability. *I think. I feel. I believe. I love. I hate.* Speaking in the first person extracts from us a certain homage to truth, both in its observance and avoidance.

Most of us in our writing substitute *it* for *I.* This practice is generally deceitful (unless one is writing fiction). The *it* style excuses the absence of feeling. Feeling is not accepted as a critical component of any truth worth seeking.

Appeals court judges subjectively make up their minds early on, then search for case law precedents later to support conclusions long foregone. Their opinions are written in the *it*, not *I*, style so they may appear scholarly, logical, and devoid of cant—as if their mothers, fathers, teachers, friends, peers hadn't begun framing opinions for them in preschool. As if the lawyers who stand before the bench needn't believe that much more comes into play than the facts and the law. As if the class, race, gender, personality, and family background of the berobed, august, elevated judge don't count as well.

Writers of nonfiction, from news copy to college textbooks, likewise hide behind *it*, claiming for their assertions an indefinable, unachievable objectivity. Perhaps, in a counterpart to truth-in-lending laws, writers should be required under some truth-in-writing statute, to write in the first-person singular—or, if not, at least required like cigarette makers to print a warning: "This writing constitutes opinions of the author and the author's view alone of the facts averred."

It is safe to assume that if Billy did not know of Nelson Mandela, he had never heard of Medgar Evers or the Middle Passage or Ethiopia B.C. If true, Billy can have no possible idea of who he is or how he came to be who he thinks he is. And if he is lost, so must I be as well, keeping small anguished company in our race before a flickering memory's light from a golden age long past. No bellows' breath for its faltering flame. No statues. No monuments. No legends. No lore. No tonic of dark immortality to brace the soul. No explanations from the masters of global information. Only silence to my needs.

So inured are blacks to the unservicableness of our substituted selves that we can scarcely ascribe responsibility for our predicament, or know in any concrete way that we *have* a predicament. Only some persistent, nonspecific, dull, subliminal self-doubt.

And this is not solely an American phenomenon.

———

Are there any questions? Silence.

Hazel, my wife, grew up in the Caribbean and learned mathematics from the English colonizers of her vegetal isle by calculating the distance from Edinburgh to Liverpool to London.

Questions? Still faces.

Girls and boys in school uniform read aloud from their readers of foreign never-seen flowers called daffodils and buttercups. See these flowers raised to a status above the uncelebrated hibiscus and yellow bells that bloom gloriously through windows opened to warm trade winds. Study Norway's fjords. Not Trinidad's rivers. Late, as well, to the knowledge of St. Kitts's own rain forest, which was never mentioned in school.

My, how well deported you boys and girls are. How many in class have read our assignments about the Thirty Years' War and the Wars of the Roses and the Punic this and the Pyrrhic that?

———

A score of hands bob and flutter. One hundred fifty years before, one hundred fifty miles to the west, slaves in Haiti had won their freedom by defeating the sixty-thousand-man army of Napoleon Bonaparte. This, never told to class.

Any questions? Oh my! What nice boys and girls.

————

It was August. It was hot and humid and the Mall was swarming with tourists. The mentor was uncertain what to do next. He was standing toward the center of the plane between the Capitol building and the Washington Monument with Billy looking up at him, a puzzled expression on his face. The mentor did not look down, vaguely embarrassed by his indecision. It was hard to put a name to what he was feeling: a mild fraying sensation, some indefinable otherness gnawing around the edges of his thoughts. Billy looked at him intently, waiting for the mentor to speak.

They were standing within sight of the Arts and Industries Building. The mentor noticed the building but gave it little thought, dismissing it as a storage facility of some sort. Stuck back in the rear of the building that tourists almost never visited was a lone small exhibit on black artists who are also scholars. This exhibit plus another on African American quilt making, a world away at the Anacostia Museum, marked the Smithsonian Institution's last resting place for Congressman John Lewis's dream of a federally supported African American museum on the Mall.

In 1988 Lewis, the former civil rights leader, joined the late congressman Mickey Leland in rallying the Congressional Black Caucus behind separate pieces of legislation that would establish an African American museum. Leland's vision was to have the funds privately raised, Lewis's to place the museum under the Smithsonian umbrella. Immediately questions were raised. Could the necessary millions be generated within the black community for a privately funded facility? And, would the Smithsonian be a wise choice to administer an African American museum, given its own clouded record on racial matters? Although plans for a Native American Smithsonian museum had moved ahead smoothly, Michael I. Heyman, the new head of the Smithsonian, who had come on board in 1995, appeared to answer the latter question by publicly questioning the need for ethnic-specific museums. So it was not surprising that many of the blacks involved had doubts about the all-white Smithsonian brain trust's ability to design, build, and administer a national museum on the experience of blacks in America.

> *But the Smithsonian is far from being a bastion of racial tolerance. As recently as 1989, its minority hiring practices came under the scrutiny of a congressional investigation, which concluded that minorities were grossly underrepresented in its upper echelons. . . . And it's worth mentioning that the Museum of Natural History's Africa hall has been shut down, in part because of its racist depictions.* —Ta-Nehisi Coates, *Washington City Paper*

Fearing that a Mall museum project would dry up funds for African American museums around the country that blacks *did* control, the African American Museum Association demanded that Lewis's legislation include fifty million dollars for *their* facilities. This rendered the legislation unpalatable to a Republican-controlled Congress. The whole matter then died quietly of politics and Senator Jesse Helms, the Republican from North Carolina, who would not allow a discussion of the proposal on the floor of the U.S. Senate.

The mentor knew nothing about any of this. Sadly, though, he knew as much as just about every American, black or white.

———

Billy lived in Southeast, only twenty minutes by subway from where they stood, but the mentor would drive him home today. Cars with license plates of all colors lined the Mall's side streets, and the mentor had had no easy time finding a space to park. The nation's capital was a largely black city, but the mentor and Billy could see no blacks from where they were. Although no hint of it passed between them, they felt as if the people from their neighborhoods had been notified not to come to the Mall on Saturdays—as if they, and not the tourists around them, had come from some far-off place.

"I'm hot."

The mentor looked toward the north side of the Mall. "Why don't we go there?"

"What is it?"

"It's an art museum."

Billy did not appear convinced.

"It's air conditioned."

"Awright."

They negotiated tourists moving sideways to their course, crossed a single-lane side street, and stood before the National Gallery of Art.

Washington is a city of varied cultural treasures, all open to the public, free of charge and paid for by the taxpayer. A branch of the Smithsonian museum system, the National Gallery houses a collection of more than one hundred thousand works of art and has received roughly a billion dollars in federal funds during the past twenty years, much of it for expansion. Of the public buildings that ring the Mall, the two that comprise the National Gallery seem the oddest companions, the staid senior West Building made even grayer by I. M. Pei's pinkish sharp-angled trapezoid beside it.

The original gallery had been erected at a time when buildings with soaring vaulted ceilings were intended to instill in their visitors a rich measure of humility.

"Have you been here before?" Billy, no longer bored, gazed up into the atrium, eyes wide.

"Once before, when I was in high school."

Inside and between the rooms where the ornately framed paintings hung, traffic moved at a contemplative pace with viewers standing motionless for long periods in front of canvases of a size Billy had not anticipated. Whistler, Sargent, Homer, Wyeth, Warhol.

The mentor and Billy caught the pace and slowly became impressed by the great works. They moved from room to room, spelling themselves on backless benches centered in the huge chambers.

"You like that?"

It was a Jackson Pollock modern piece. The mentor looked at the canvas steadily. "I don't know if I do or not."

"Is that art?" Billy was looking at an array of twenty-five Andy Warhol soup can labels.

"Not to me."

Billy stopped before a wall-sized abstract of geometric boxes and lyrical applications of color. The pattern, unlike any he'd seen, held his attention. "I like this one."

Other patterns, ones to which he had already acclimated in

his short life, he would seem to find altogether unremarkable. There were pictures of men standing, men sitting, men riding, women posing (elaborately dressed), women reposing (fleshily undressed), children with children, children with dogs, families doing family things. Scenes of people in frames. Scenes of people, motionless, starring at the scenes of people in the frames. Nothing here seemed out of the ordinary to Billy or to the mentor or to the people who continued to move slowly from room to room.

All was as it always had been at the National Gallery of Art. All of the framed faces were white. Virtually all the patrons peering at them were white as well. Only the guards in blue uniforms were black.

Of course, there were the mentor and Billy. And a lone black presence Billy could not have known about: a small landscape, *Abraham's Oak*, painted by Henry Ossawa Tanner (1859–1937), hanging in an obscure corner.

> *If my father lived so much abroad it was owing to the fact that he felt the white people in America were not ready to face acceptance of the colored races, especially the Negro race. He believed this acceptance would eventually be worked out through education and equal opportunity, though it might take many years.*
> —Jesse Ossawa Tanner Le Douhet, France, 1969

Tanner, disillusioned with America, had sailed for Europe in 1891 to pursue his career in France, with perhaps his most important work to follow from stops in North Africa and the Middle East. His oil landscape was the only painting by an African American artist on display. Nothing of Lewis or Bearden or

Catlett or Barthé or Lawrence. Nothing. Only Tanner, home again and alone, would have seen the irony.

In the foyer on the way out, the mentor saw on the wall a large gilded frame encasing the oval black-and-white photographs of the gallery's board of directors. With small expectation, not unlike that which attends the purchase of a lottery ticket, he looked quickly for a break in the visages' uniformity. He found none.

———————

"Did any black people fight in the Vietnam War?"

Billy and the mentor sat on a slatted Mall bench just across from the side street running in front of the West Building. It was late afternoon. The air had cooled markedly during their time in the gallery. The sun's low angle made the grass appear greener than it had before.

"Why did you ask *that*?"

"You know. Down there." Billy was pointing down the Mall beyond the Washington Monument. "Where the black wall has all of the names on it."

"The Vietnam War Memorial."

"Yeah. Were there black people in that war?"

"Yes. Why?"

"There musta been a hundred people at that wall down there. But I didn't see no black people."

"A whole lot of black people fought in that war and a whole lot of black people died in that war."

"How come then all the people down there are white?"

"I don't know. Seems like mostly all the people we've seen today are white."

The mentor thought about what he had said. He could remember seeing fewer than ten blacks during the whole of the day, and they were all attached to white people, as if a notice had specified that blacks coming to the Mall on Saturdays should not come unattended. A few, about Billy's age, the mentor had spotted in integrated school groups. There had been three others in their mid-to-late twenties: a black woman wearing thick owlish glasses, strolling hand-in-hand with a bookish-looking white man, and two black men with white women. One of the men had walked directly toward the mentor and Billy on a narrow footpath near the Lincoln Memorial. As the four came abreast, Billy was forced to step to his right onto the grass. The mentor looked at the black man but the black man did not look at him.

They sat for a while in silence. Billy hadn't known how to interpret the mentor's uncharacteristic quiet.

"Are you ready to go?" Billy asked, more a pleading than a question.

"Come on. I'll drop you at home."

The mentor thought he could come again to the Mall for a march or some activity of the sort. Otherwise he would not come, with or without Billy. Little about the day had made him feel good. A pall of vague inescapable foreignness weighed upon him. His sense of rejection was not conscious but dully there nonetheless.

Who am I? Just who the hell am I?

It is life's core question, isn't it? *Who am I?* In the existential sense, it is the question that cannot be answered. One evening my daughter Khalea, age eight at the time, asked, "Daddy, how can I know I am here and you are there? Do you know what I mean?"

"Yes, I know," I told her. From inside her young walled consciousness, she had asked the unanswerable. I smiled unhelpfully. She smiled. She had been more amused than troubled by the conundrum.

The *who-am-I?* question the mentor asks is not Khalea's question. The mentor's question *has* answers. Answers as essential to the human psyche as food and water are to the body. Answers without which no social progress is possible. Answers that societies alloy with myth when need be. Frail answers made sacred over time by mindless catechism. Real answers that the weaker aspects of us all can seize upon like flotation devices on a tall sea.

Truths. Half-truths. Unsupportable myths. Outrageous lies. Polished together into history. Statuary totems dotting the urban landscape at close intervals, sentinels for those who know a society's measure of itself to be tabulated largely from the feats, real and imagined, of the long dead.

Who am I? the mentor asks as he is surrounded by the statuary of others, the sentinels of others, which were put there to comfort them and mock him, to take them to *their* truth and deflect him from his, to encompass those others and imprison him. In every central park.

Posturing on pedestals.

Atop rearing steeds.

Majestically seated.

Could it be that they are chanting? *This is who we are. This is who we are.* Standing there as high as buildings in some unending spasm of state-funded narcissism. What succor could the mentor find here before Lincoln, who had thought that the idea of shipping all blacks back to Africa was, at the very least, worthy of exploration? What emotion should he feel before Thomas Jefferson, who had owned him as chattel?

Although the mentor had never read Jefferson's *Notes on the State of Virginia*, published in 1785, he intuited well their meaning on his outing with Billy that Saturday.

———

Sir Eric Williams, the Trinidadian historian, has written much about Jefferson and the Atlantic slave trade:

> Jefferson regarded the Negro in America as inferior not only to the white man but also to the Amerindian, whose drawings, paintings, carving and oratory proved, in his view, the existence of a germ in their minds which only needed cultivation. But he found the Negro incapable of any thought above the level of plain narration, without even an elementary trait of painting or sculpture. They were gifted with accurate ears for tune and time, but it was yet to be proved whether they were equal to the composition of a more extensive run of melody, or of complicated harmony. With misery enough among them, there was no poetry. Phyllis Wheatley's poems he considered beneath the dignity of criticism. . . . Thus did Jefferson, without knowing it, dismiss the Benin bronzes, the marvels of Zimbabwe, Negro music, and the poetry of Aimé Césaire and Leopold Sedar Senghor.
>
> . . . But the differences between the two races, especially that of colour, led Jefferson to advocate the total removal of the Negroes, after emancipation, "beyond the reach of mixture."

My dear Miss Sally Hemings, has the man no shame?
I had thought about Sally Hemings while signing books in a

small black history museum in an inner-city neighborhood of Richmond, Virginia, my hometown. I had visited the red-brick two-story colonial building often as a teen when it served as the Rosa Bowser Community Library.

On a break from signing, I had moved animatedly through the three downstairs exhibition rooms with Hazel and Khalea before stopping in front of a framed sepia portrait of a Virginia slave family. The shadowy portrait had been printed from a nineteenth-century daguerreotype.

The father and mother sat on a plank bench wearing frayed church-going apparel: he with curled satin lapels sewn to an ill-fitting jacket, she in a dark brocaded fabric with a rent straining open below the bodice. They were flanked by a son and daughter who appeared to be in their mid-twenties. Behind them, standing uncomfortably for the long sulphur-lighted exposure, were three young men and a woman, all formally, if poorly, dressed.

I was arrested by their eyes, trained on me through the camera's lens. The magnetic stare seemed to bind them as a family, as if they were tenaciously defending the scattered remains of battered dignity. The children wore the same stern opaque expression of challenge. The father and mother, leaning toward each other and gazing out in mournful tenderness, seemed to reveal more in their countenance than they might have wished. Pride, anger, despair, searing shame mixed in the father's eyes.

The husband and wife had the rich black skin common to the Wolof of Senegal. The young man on the bench to the right of the father, the standing woman, and two of her brothers were similarly dark-complected with the well-formed features of their parents. The girl, seated beside her mother, and the son in the rear to the right looked very different, but very much a part of the family at the same time. Their eyes may have been gray or blue. Their skin was fair. Their hair was very nearly straight.

I looked again for a time into the pleading eyes of the mother: *These are my children.* And then for a longer while into the embarrassed, pained eyes of the father: *This, even still, is my family.*

My wife and child and I stood in silence before the picture of the Virginia slave family for a long while, moved by its tableau of hurts. We hadn't before fully contemplated what slave ownership could expand to mean. *We were theirs to do with as they pleased.* I had pictured the rape of our women. I had not, in my mind's eye, pictured the women as daughters. I had not pictured them as wives.

The girl, seated by her mother, stared at me.

The difference [between the races] is fixed in nature. . . . And is this difference of no importance? . . . Are not the fine mixtures of red and white, the expressions of every passion by greater or less suffusions of colour in the one, preferable to the eternal monotony, which reigns in the countenances, that immovable veil of black which covers all the emotions of the other race? Add to these, flowing hair, a more elegant symmetry of form, their [blacks] own judgment in favour of the whites, declared by their preference of them, as uniformly as is the preference of the Oranootan [orangutan] for the black women over those of his own species. —Thomas Jefferson, *Notes on the State of Virginia*

I thought of Sally Hemings, another light-skinned slave who was the half sister of Thomas Jefferson's wife, Martha. When Jefferson, forty-three, was serving in Paris in 1786 as ambassador to France, Sally, fourteen, was ordered by Jefferson to accompany his youngest daughter, Mary, on the long sea voyage. After returning to Monticello with Jefferson in 1789, Sally bore, while living on the estate, at least five children, several of whom were said to strikingly resemble Jefferson, and at least one of whom, Eston, was later conclusively proved through DNA comparisons to have been Jefferson's son.

The nation's third president, author of the Declaration of Independence, and rutting statesman would pinion slave child Sally captive beneath him for a period that would run to thirty-eight years, never to set her free. Lubricious with heat by night, writing by day.

Had he a caprice to, he could have killed Sally and faced no consequences. He could have done *anything* to *any* of them, for they were but chattel about whose forebears he had apparently learned nothing from the works of Herodotus or Diodorus.

> *Comparing them by their faculties of memory, reason, and imagination, it appears to me, that in memory they are equal to the whites; in reason much inferior, as I think one could scarcely be found capable of tracing and comprehending the investigations of Euclid; and that in imagination they are dull, tasteless, and anomalous.* —Thomas Jefferson, *Notes on the State of Virginia*

In another place and time the middle-aged Jefferson's sexual plundering of Sally would have been described as rape. She had begun with him as a child, and even well into her majority she would have no choice in the matter. He was the father of American liberty, who had indeed taken plenty with a young woman he had selected from a pool of human property he once described in animal terms.

> *They secrete less by the kidneys, and more by the glands of the skin, which gives them a very strong and disagreeable odour. . . . They are at least as brave, and more adventuresome. But this may perhaps proceed from a want of forethought, which prevents their seeing a danger till it be present. . . . Their griefs are transient.*
>
> —Thomas Jefferson, *Notes on the State of Virginia*

It is often argued in Jefferson's defense that it is unfair to hold his behavior with regard to race to modern standards, that after all he was "a man of his time." But who isn't? Thomas Paine?

What about Genghis Khan? In the year 1220 A.D., the Mongol khan and eighty thousand horsemen burst from the steppes of Mongolia through the gates of Samarkand and proceeded to lay waste to central Asia's greatest cities—Bukhara, Urgench, Balkh, Merv, Nishapur, Herat, Ghazni. By the year 1280, Mongol rule reached from the Yellow Sea to the Mediterranean. Before Genghis's death at age sixty, his armies had subjugated millions and established an empire eclipsed in scale only by the British empire of the nineteenth century. As the first ruler of united Mongolia, he is thought of by Mongolians much the same way as most Americans think of George Washington. In the West, of course, he is remembered as a ruthless scourge. But he was every bit as much a man of his time as Jefferson was of his.

For that matter, the same specious excuse can be offered for Ataturk or Franco or Lenin or Mao or Hitler. All of them committed great wrongs within permissive if not supportive environments. But this cannot be allowed to render their heinous wrongs any less reprehensible.

For wasn't the practice of slavery at least as serious a system of human-rights wrongs as the Nazi holocaust? Did not the holocaust of slavery last longer—indeed, 234 years longer? Did it not claim at least twice as many lives, in the Middle Passage alone? Did it not savagely eviscerate the emotional core of a whole race of people on three continents? In raising any defense of Jefferson, a powerful American cog in slavery's long-grinding machine, are we not then subscribing to Jefferson's view that a black life has lesser value, black suffering an inconsequential significance? *Their griefs are transient.*

Does not the continued unremarked American deification of Jefferson tell us all how profoundly contemptuous of black sensibilities American society persists in being? How deeply, stubbornly, poisonously racist our society to this day remains?

Jefferson was a slaveholder, a racist, and—if one accepts that consent cannot be given if it cannot be denied—a rapist.

Of course, Jefferson was only unusual in that he wrote copiously for posterity about his appraisal of the traits of those he owned as chattel. Countless others of high social station, if less famous than Jefferson, committed acts no less reprehensible than his.

J. Marion Sims, for instance, is broadly recognized as the father of American gynecology. He won this distinction by improving the speculum and developing a surgical technique to correct small tears between the vagina and the bladder. Dr. Sims's procedure was tried on white women only after he had experimented with it repeatedly on slave women, without their volition and without anesthesia.

While there were those like Thomas Paine who found the whole business of the slave trade abhorrent, they were far outnumbered by slaveholders who, among other things, forced female slaves into sexual service. As Frederick Douglass wrote in *Narrative of the Life of Frederick Douglass, An American Slave* (1845):

> This occurrence took place very soon after I went to live with my old master, and under the following circumstances. Aunt Hester went out one night,—where or for what I do not know,—and happened to be absent when my master desired her presence. He had ordered her not to go out evenings, and warned her that she must never let him catch her in company with a young man, who was paying attention to her belonging to Colonel Lloyd. The young man's name was Ned Roberts, generally called Lloyd's Ned. Why master was so careful of her, may be safely left to conjecture. She was a woman of noble form, and of graceful proportions, having very few equals, and fewer superiors, in personal appearance, among the colored or white woman of our neighborhood.
>
> Aunt Hester had not only disobeyed his orders in going out, but had been found in company with Lloyd's Ned; which circumstance, I found from what he said while whipping her, was the chief offense. Had he been a man of pure morals, himself, he might have been thought interested in protecting the innocence of my Aunt; but those who knew him will not suspect him of such virtue. Before he commenced whipping Aunt Hester, he took her to the kitchen, and stripped her from the neck to the waist, leaving her neck, shoulders, and back, entirely naked. He then told her to cross her hands, calling her at the same time a "d——d b——h." After crossing her hands, he tied them with a strong rope, and led her to a stool under a large hook in a joist, put in for the purpose. He made her get upon the stool, and tied her hands to the hook. She now stood fair for his infernal purpose. Her arms were stretched up at their full length, so that she stood upon the

ends of her toes. He then said to her, "Now, you d——d b——h. I'll learn you how to disobey my orders" and after rolling up her sleeves, he commenced to lay on the heavy cowskin, and soon the warm, red blood (amid heart-rending shrieks from her, and horrid oaths from him) came dripping to the floor.

The long impenetrable shadow of slavery covers our national society still, leaving one community with flawed gods and another with no gods at all.

Now, here they all were in a pantheon of the laughing dead, immortalized in stone from the public tax quarry, gods looking down upon the heads of their pilgrim subjects among whom were seen, for the gods' eternal amusement, those whom the gods had deemed subhuman. The whole business had seemed narcissistic, however, only to the left-out and unremembered. Truth be told, such acts of self-celebration were as natural as breathing. They had been practiced in every human society as far back as anthropology would reach, a necessary part of any salubrious human existence.

———

And Billy's mentor might have thought—

They have taken my *tax dollars and bought only what* they *need.*

Since this nation's inception, taxpayers—white, black, brown—have spent billions on museums, monuments, memorials, parks, centers for the performing arts, festivals, and commemorative occasions. Billions more have been spent on the publication of history texts, arts texts, magazines, newspapers, and history journals. Formulaic television and large-screen historical fiction treatments virtually defy count.

Almost none of this spending, building, unveiling, and publishing has been addressed to the needs of Americans who are not white.

They have taken my *tax dollars and bought only what* they *need.*

And, indeed, *needs* are what we are talking about here. If human beings, over time, when free to perform or not perform a given act, in fact invariably perform it, it is safe to assume that they *need* to perform it. How else could we explain the American expenditure of billions of tax dollars on stone likenesses or London's refurbishment of the Albert Memorial or the maintenance of Lenin's waxen corpse or the labor-intensive carving of the towering volcanic rock statues of Easter Island?

Ancestor worship is not alone the exotic preoccupation of quaint people mired in superstition in some remote corner of the world. Larger-than-life evidence of its industrialized-world variants can be seen in virtually every public park in America.

George Washington is the quintessential American public ancestor. Americans worship him before an obelisk in Washington, a statue in Baltimore, a square in New York, an engraving on the dollar, and Stuart prints hanging from coast to coast. (Washington couldn't have known that the obelisk to be dedicated in memory of him, on February 21, 1885, would be the world's largest replica of a 3,500-year-old monument to the Egyptian sun god.) Obviously Americans, like all other people, *need* to worship their ancestors, either privately before cracked sepia photographs of stiff unsmiling long-dead kin or publicly at shrines like Mount Vernon, George Washington's home on the shore of Virginia's Potomac River.

Trouble is, George Washington is not *my* ancestor, private or public. He *owned* my ancestors, abused them as chattel and willed them to his wife, Martha, upon his death. I and mine need to know about George and Martha but, assuredly, we do not need to revere them. Indeed, psychically we cannot afford to revere them.

They have taken my *tax dollars and bought only what* they *need.* Billy's mentor had thought nothing of the kind. He knew nothing of Africa before the Atlantic slave trade or since. He knew little of his people's contemporary history, and there was nothing on the Mall to suggest to him that they had any. He only knew what was ordinary and all around him in a seamless commemoration of white accomplishment. The sight had not made him angry. He hadn't information enough for anger. If he felt anything, it was a bleakness he thought to stem from some personal inadequacy.

Blacks need to remember who we are, not remember with others who *they* are.

> *The devil white man cut these black people off from all knowledge of their own kind, and cut them off from any knowledge of their own language, religion, and past culture, until the black man in America was the earth's only race of people who had absolutely no knowledge of his true identity.*
> —*The Autobiography of Malcolm X*

We, like others, need to define ourselves, to place our lives in a long-term linear intergenerational context. We, like others, need to celebrate ourselves by seeing ourselves celebrated. We, like others, need to stare at objects that can help us discover reflections of ourselves in an idealized past.

That's really what it's all about, isn't it? Remembering. The human's innate need to remember one's self before one's own time. Distantly before. And reassuringly.

What then was I doing visiting George Washington's Mount Vernon many years ago with Hazel?

Confused?

Confessedly. How can any American who isn't white not be?

———

Hazel and I walked toward Mount Vernon's outbuildings and came upon a small grassy square enclosed by a white wooden fence. The tide of tourists had remained in the white colonnaded mansion, and we were alone until we sighted a black man in livery walking in the direction of a small clapboard building in the cul-de-sac near the main house.

"Sir!" I called out.

The man stopped and turned. He was no more than thirty feet away.

"What is this area for?"

He might have answered but didn't. Instead he walked toward us, saying nothing until he'd closed on us completely. "This is where the slaves are buried," he said solemnly. He hadn't said "George Washington's slaves," simply "the slaves." I liked his choice of words, and the three of us gave each other comradely looks.

George Washington was a third-generation slaveholder, who with Martha owned more than three hundred slaves. He prized them particularly; as a signal of wealth in his world, such property exceeded gold and real estate. He had once written to a fellow planter urging that he send him strong slaves in good health who were not "addicted to running away." At the end of the Revolutionary War, he cordoned the beaches with soldiers to prevent runaway slaves who had fought with the British from leaving America with the redcoats.

———

The liveried gentleman took his leave. Hazel and I stood motionless on the periphery of the plot, saying nothing, reluctant to tread over the unmarked graves of those whose anonymous sufferings we could scarcely fathom.

I am not a churchgoing man. Strangled in the vines of form and choked with ritual Christians, Sunday service held no appeal for me as a child. When my parents released me from compulsory attendance, I would never return. In my view, religion is best practiced out of doors, in nature's cathedral of miracles where spirits and the arts of heaven mingle unencumbered. The spirits were present on the tiny unmarked parcel at Mount Vernon that early autumn afternoon.

Hazel and I stood for a long while in complete silence. Words would have marred, much as they misserve this inadequate telling of what we felt. We had been touched by wearied souls calling, in a language ethereal as morning mist, from the near realm that awaits us all.

These were *our* ancestors and, alone behind an old wooden outbuilding, my wife and I had wordlessly worshiped with them on that clear crisp afternoon.

3

RACE TO CLASS
TO RACE

If there is a Fatherhood of God that is indivisible, then there is a Brotherhood of Man that is not subject to degrees and fractions. Therefore, the persistence of class stratification is unacceptable morally, divisive socially, obstructionist economically and a source of tension which, if not removed, will inevitably provoke social instability.

—Michael Manley, *The Politics of Change*

T HE WINDS COME and go, year in, year out, performing their seasonal ripples of pace and direction, registering little on the timeless forest. The mammoth redwoods appear impervious to such forces. Away at the top, the fronds flutter and dance on the gentlest of breezes. Once or so in a season, the small branches to which the eye-catching leaves are attached can be seen to sway slowly, almost imperceptibly, before resuming, on the winds' pauses, their natural places. The steep angle of view and distance from the ground mix to hypnotic effect, creating an illusion, not of life, but of change: change as imminent as the gay motion of the tossing fronds. But the trees' boughs and coarse trunks remain utterly still. Against the strongest gusts, they are as still as the ground on which the old trees commit themselves to their immovable berths.

America's socioeconomic gaps between the races remain, like the aged redwoods rooted in a forest floor, going nowhere, seen but not disturbed, simulating infinity, normalcy. Static.

High infant mortality. Low income. High unemployment. Substandard education. Capital incapacity. Insurmountable credit barriers. High morbidity. Below-average life span. Overrepresentation in prison—and on death row. Each a cause and/or a consequence of a disabling poverty—of means and spirit—that has shackled all too many entire black family trees since the Emancipation Proclamation, as if the painful fates had been painted onto some antebellum canvas that had dried mean during slavery. Modern observers now look at the canvas as if its subjects were to be forever fixed in a foreordained inequality.

Of the many reasons for this inequality, chief of course is the seemingly incurable virus of *de facto* discrimination that continues to poison relations between the races at all levels.

In average income, African Americans continue to trail far behind Asian Americans and whites, and have recently fallen into last place behind Hispanic Americans. Contemporary discrimination alone does not explain the persistence of these income gaps. Another culprit is a mutant form of the coarse and visible old discrimination. This sneaky and invisible culprit can be called conditioned expectation.

We hardly ever in life exceed the expectations set for us by the general society. Some of us are conditioned to excel. Others are conditioned to fail. Few of us, however, are conditioned to give much conscious thought to where the bar has been set for us.

There are, to be sure, exceptions to this rule of conditioned expectation. There are always those special few who achieve (or fail) against all odds. There are those, like me, whose families successfully defy mainstream society's low expectation of us. The exceptions, however, would not be numerous enough to allow the closing of the income gap, even if the coarse and tangible old brand of discrimination were to go tomorrow into some period of long-term miracle remission.

This is so because a static, unarticulated, insidious racial conditioning, to which all Americans are subject, lifts the high-expectation meritless (Dan Quayle comes to mind here) and, more often than not, locks down in a permanent class hell the natively talented but low-expectation black. The gap mocks the efforts of the best of us, black and white, like some ageless yawning crevasse that separates the perennially privileged on their gilded higher ground from those who learn from birth to expect and therefore to reach for little.

———

More than twenty-five years have passed but I remember her well. Her name was Anna. She was twenty-eight years old and living in a Boston public housing tenement when I met her. Her factory job required her to punch in no later than eight in the morning. Anna rose every day at 5:30 A.M., performed cold-water ablutions, ate toast made of day-old bread, roused her two children, and, leaving them to fend for themselves, headed out in darkness by 6:30 A.M. to catch a train and two buses in order to arrive on time at her place of work. The children, Sarah, twelve, and Robert, seven, having gone back to sleep, would wake themselves at seven, wash and dress, then eat a cold cereal breakfast left for them on the table in the tiny kitchen by Anna. By eight o'clock, the children would make their way down three flights of a dark stairwell before separating on the sidewalk to walk in opposite directions to their schools, six blocks away in his case and ten blocks in hers.

It had been unseasonably cold that fall. The deep chill had

preceded by days, if not weeks, the scheduled arrival of heat from the city's housing authority to the tenement apartments. Thus it was to a cold space that Anna would return from work at six on those October evenings. More often than not the lightbulbs above the stairwell landings would be out. This gave her a considerable feeling of unease, given the social and physical condition of the neighborhood in which she and her children had little choice but to live.

The foyer, which smelled of urine, had two rows of mailboxes, all long ago rifled and mangled so far out of alignment that the metal doors would no longer lock. Not infrequently, gunfire from the street below could be heard during the night in Anna's and Sarah's bedrooms. The living room doubled as Robert's.

In winter, arriving home from work after dark, Anna would approach the metal door to her third-floor apartment with an apprehensiveness eased only when she found her children safely home from school. It was a daily anxiety that, although not conscious, compounded with the long workday to claim what remaining store of energy she had. It would be seven o'clock before she would ask both of them about their homework assignments. Her questions were perfunctory. Having left school at sixteen, Anna had little if any capacity to help her children with schoolwork they couldn't understand or even to check the results of work that they could.

By nine o'clock, Anna would climb into bed and lie sleepless with nameless worry. The streets were dangerous. Gangs, for many boys, served as the only families they had. Recently she had begun to be afraid for Robert. Soon she would not be able to confine him to the apartment. She would lose control of him to the streets where prospects for black male survival were poor. She was no less concerned about Sarah—not so much for her safety, as with Robert, but instead about whether Sarah would become pregnant in high school as Anna had, and lose what small chance she had of getting *out*.

Anna was very tired. Her weariness was tinged in no small measure with guilt. She wanted her children, above all, to get an "education," though for her the word was little more than a mantra. Her supervisor had been unsympathetic to her appeals for time off to visit her children's schools for meetings with their teachers. She so seldom got to go that she felt ill at ease with the school officials on the few occasions she encountered them.

The simple truth was that she had no idea what was going on in her children's schools (and if one could believe Jonathan Kozol, author of *Death at an Early Age* and *Savage Inequalities*, very little was). She was just so tired. She thought for a moment that she should check to see if the children had clean clothes for school before dozing off. But she could not pull herself back from the edge of sleep.

Anna did not own a car. She did not own a clothes washer or a dryer or a vacuum cleaner or a dishwasher. The only "luxuries" to be found in her small apartment were the telephone in the living room, a clock-radio in her bedroom, and a small-screen black-and-white television with a bent clothes hanger for an antenna. Her lack of belongings rendered her life not so much unpleasant—well, that too—but unmanageable to an extent that drove her to the verge of panic. Every necessary ordinary little task required a trip. A trip required a bus. A bus took time. Time she didn't have. Her building had no washing machines, so she had to take a bus to the Laundromat. This chore alone claimed a large part of her Saturdays. Grocery shopping was much the same, except that she could not transport five to seven bags of groceries on a bus. She had to take a taxi home which she could not afford. The shopping routinely claimed the balance of her Saturdays. Even the small task of getting enough exact change in dollars and coins on Sundays for a week's worth of bus fares and school lunches seemed a large matter when added to a to-do list already too long. Or getting to the check-cashing store (with its exorbitant service charges) on payday Fridays before closing time. Or buying clothing at discount stores. Indeed, she saw this job as particularly thankless. Her children wanted designer clothes they had seen advertised on television. Robert had once become disagreeable in a store when she had refused to buy for him a pair of basketball shoes that would have cost her a week's salary. In that same store, she had seen another spent mother yell at her four-year-old son and raise her hand as if to strike the boy. Anna did not approve, but she understood as others may not have.

In this particular respect, she had taken to worrying about herself. She was beginning to have intermittent feelings of terror. She strove to be a good mother but she had neither the time nor the resources necessary. Oftener than not she hadn't the emotional wherewithal to focus on certain discrete elements of her children's needs.

Although they were of the right weight for their ages, she knew little about nutrition, or that her failure to provide it adequately might have already permanently damaged her children's learning ability. Once, on a visit to a neighborhood clinic with Sarah, ill with a virus, Anna read the illustrated charts on the wall and experienced the familiar surge of terror. There had been a nutrition poster with three suggested balanced meals pictured in color. Another poster urged periodic medical and dental checkups for children. None of this had Anna been able to do.

A dental chart on an opposite wall urged parents to supervise the brushing of their children's teeth. Anna felt another pang. She seldom was even home to see Sarah and Robert brush their teeth. Her mind had then begun to race and fasten onto the question of whether her children had cavities and how many. She had no answer, and this caused her to visibly slump in the waiting room chair.

The other side of Anna's periodic bouts of panic was a now almost generalized despondency that deepened with certain sound and sight associations. The word *parents* depressed her because it sounded normative and she was all alone beneath her burden. Similarly, the terms

PTA,
library,
homework,
conference,
reading

depressed her by reminding her of things she ought to be doing, wanted to be doing, but simply had no time to do, no time at all. The sight of braces bothered her, and particularly when they were on girls' teeth. A girl's braces told Anna that the girl's mother had plenty of time and plenty of money. She hated braces. They mocked her straits, glinting like silver laces around the teeth of the carefree. Here she was, without a clue as to the state of her children's dental health, and other children were wearing braces—and had more money in their pockets than Anna had in hers.

Once, Anna had been asked by Sarah's English teacher to come to school on a Saturday to meet with a team of lawyers from Washington who were evaluating the Boston schools' use of federal money under the Title I program. The program's principal purpose was to provide compensatory assistance to students in grades K through 12 who had fallen below grade level in math and reading. Sarah, who should have been reading on a seventh-grade level, had recently fallen behind.

Title I regulations required, among other things, the active involvement of parents in programs assisting their children. The people in Washington who wrote the laws had time to spend in their children's schools. They must have thought that Anna too could make time to spend in her children's. But, as was the case with the vast majority of the working poor, time was not Anna's to make. It was her supervisor's, and he was not sympathetic.

The strain stamped on Anna's face must have been apparent to the three lawyers seated across from her. As a young lawyer, I served on a similar panel once for the Lawyers Committee for Civil Rights Under Law. We traveled throughout the country checking to see that the statutory conditions for Title I assistance were being met by school districts receiving funds. There were eight or so such conditions, including parental participation. Everywhere we went, we were told that parent involvement had been "effective" or "useful" or "constructive." But it soon became apparent that the various programs had received only minimal involvement from parents whose explanations did not differ very much from Anna's.

They simply had no time. What's more, as one could plainly enough see from the look on Anna's face, poor people with grade-school educations are often intimidated in discussions with professional educators about abstruse rubbish like "comparative principles and methods of pedagogy."

The lawyers were droning on to Anna about . . .

I will never get to the laundry.

. . . fulfillment of statutory conditions . . .

The milk will be gone at the Safeway.

. . . promulgated under Title I . . .

What in the world are they talking about and what does it have to do with Sarah and Robert?

Sarah's English teacher, Ms. Cooper, sat beside Anna in the meeting. She was white and younger than Anna. Her suit was sober but stylish. Her face was well scrubbed and free of worry lines. She wore braces on teeth that appeared not to need them.

Anna did not feel good about herself in this discussion. The three lawyers, one of whom was black, spoke among themselves and to Ms. Cooper in a grammar Anna recognized as better than hers. This made Anna try to speak in a way she would not have ordinarily. Her struggle to mimic the way they spoke *must be obvious to them*, she thought. *Not just obvious but comical.* This realization shamed her and she fell quiet.

"How many times have you been able to come to the Title I parent meetings at school in the last year, Mrs. Brown?" asked one of the white lawyers. Anna had thought he was about her age. The lawyer had guessed Anna to be much older than he.

"Well, I come when I can." This was an evasion. The school had originally scheduled the meetings for late afternoon beginning just after class dismissal. Anna and several other parents with children in the program would be either still at work at that time or just leaving work. So the meetings had been moved to Saturdays, but that hadn't boosted attendance much either.

"But just how many times?"

"I have never been to one."

"Can you tell us why?"

Anna told them about her life, in the idiom of her world, with no embarrassed fakery. She told them about the long hours spent on her job and at the Laundromat and cooking, what it was like to be alone with responsibility for her children's lives. She told them about struggling to make it on a minimum-wage paycheck. She told them everything, except that she was afraid on more than one front, that she felt trapped, that she loved her children but didn't know how to show them any exit from her own grim fate. It disturbed her to look at her children and see her life as theirs to come. But things had been this way as far back as anyone in her family could remember. They had always been poor. And she had finally come to believe that they always would be.

"Do you read with Sarah at home?" asked the other white lawyer.

"Yes, as often as I can," answered Anna wearily. *Are these people crazy? Have they listened to nothing I've said?* Anna looked at Ms. Cooper, whose expression gave away little of what she might have been thinking.

"Mrs. Brown," said the black lawyer, who was older by twenty years than anyone else in the room, "if Sarah is as bright as you are, she should have no trouble reading. Have you ever heard of the United Nations Children's Fund?"

"No, I haven't."

"Well, it's called UNICEF for short and they've come out with a report showing that nearly a billion people in the world can't read and write and that fifteen percent of the people in countries like ours are what they call functionally illiterate. This means that all these people are doomed to lives of poverty. This doesn't have to happen to your children and I know you don't want it to happen. But we've got to find ways to make this program work better."

"I see," Anna said absently.

She was somewhere else now, gone in her thoughts from what was beginning to feel like an inquisition. She pulled her large handbag from her lap and held it against her bosom like a baseball catcher's chest protector. She said nothing more.

Ms. Cooper turned her head and looked at Anna, as if for the first time. This was the longest the two had even been in the same room together. They had met once before, earlier in the year, at a parent-teacher conference. The meeting, one of thirty-three Ms. Cooper had held that day, had lasted barely ten minutes. Anna was the last parent on the schedule at 6:35 and barely made it on time. Ms. Cooper had learned little in the meeting, not even enough to remember Anna's face. By that time Sarah had fallen behind in reading proficiency, and she was further behind now. This hadn't surprised Ms. Cooper. She'd expected it, although she hadn't known why. It wasn't that Sarah was black, or at least she didn't think so. She hadn't known many blacks but she'd gone to college in the Midwest with a number of them, some of whom had done much better than she, which surprised her.

So that isn't it. Well, maybe some of it. No, I think—

She glanced again at Anna.

It's that they look so poor, act poor, talk poor. I wonder what she's thinking. Or do I have to wonder? I learned more about her and her family in the last five minutes than I'd ever known before. Her blouse is soiled.

The English teacher was in her first job after college. It had been only three years since she'd arrived in Boston. She hadn't wanted to teach, but she needed to save money for graduate school. She was hoping to attend Simmons on the Fenway.

The lawyers were talking to Ms. Cooper now about Title I program operations at the school. This gave Anna an opportunity to look directly at Ms. Cooper.

Braces. Sarah don't like her and I can see why. Sarah has never had no trouble before this year. Before this teacher. Sarah is smart. I know she is. But this teacher don't even know her.

Anna did not know that Sarah had been assigned to Ms. Cooper's class by computer. She also did not know that the school's principal considered Ms. Cooper to be one of his weakest teachers and that, computer assignment notwithstanding, students with parents likely to complain were never assigned to teachers like Ms. Cooper.

Anna had never complained, for at least two reasons: first, she hadn't the time or energy, and second, she really didn't know how to lodge a complaint, or at least, how to do it effectively. She saw her poverty as a smothering, ever darkening cell outside of which lived those like Ms. Cooper and these lawyers who seemed to have control not only over their own lives but over hers as well. She knew no one who could help her up or out in the world. She was no one to anyone who counted. Not a single teacher, lawyer, doctor, preacher, politician, bureaucrat, journalist, or higher factotum could she presume to greet by his or her given name. She was as unconnected as they came. She was an anonymous worker bee. Raw grist for the merry miller. An expendable scene-edge extra in an epic drama for which neither she nor anyone she knew had ever been shown a script. She was a registered voter who voted. She attended her Pentecostal church with her children every Sunday without fail. And Lord knows she worked hard. None of it did any good. Already Robert worried about whether he would live to manhood. And now Sarah, tied by impersonal fates to a mother who could not change their direction, their speed, or their destination. Anna had taken hope from poster art and public service ads that education could be an answer for her children, but all that had been just a mirage. Although Anna hadn't been equipped to picture it so, the generations of her family were like beads on a taut string, one end anchored in slavery, the other in oblivion.

Anna was at her wit's end to understand the forces that constricted her life choices. In some visceral way, she knew that Ms. Cooper expected Sarah to fail. But Anna thought it was only because Sarah was black. In fact, Ms. Cooper's reasons were more complex, even though she did not consciously know what her reasons were. From the moment she met Sarah, Ms. Cooper had subliminally formed a number of assumptions that affected her behavior as Sarah's teacher. Her mind's camera had registered Sarah's social indicia simultaneously in one short exposure: the clothes, the hairstyle, the bearing, the speech pattern, the skin color—

Black and poor.

Ms. Cooper linked the two while never likening poor blacks to the poor whites she had seen, though their economic status was every bit as apparent from their *look* as Sarah's was from hers. For Ms. Cooper, who'd never really thought about it, poverty *was* the black look, as if it were an innate racial characteristic. She had seen poor whites, yes, but they weren't poor because they were white. They were poor because they were either crazy or the victims of bad fortune. But no one, after all, could expect Ms. Cooper, who was not a deep thinker, to overcome the wide-ranging iconography of an American culture that had long pictured blacks and whites quite the way she saw them. She had succumbed, without a moment's struggle, to the soothing undertow of her world: poor blacks were poor because they were black.

For Anna's part, she could have no way of knowing that she and her children had been locked into the box of her economic class and sentenced to lives of privation generations ago during American slavery. Back then, the fact that she was black was, by itself, enough to seal her fate. In the time since, such fate had been realized through conditions that the cruel institution had promised to those making up the new economic subclass that slavery had mercilessly forged.

By the time I left Boston in 1975, much of the light in Robert's eyes had died. Sarah, always stronger than he, was maintaining an attractive pluckiness when last I saw her. Anna was old before she was thirty. I don't know what became of them, but the odds were not kind.

———

No nation can enslave a race of people for hundreds of years, set them free bedraggled and penniless, pit them, without assistance in a hostile environment, against privileged victimizers, and then reasonably expect the gap between the heirs of the two groups to narrow. Lines, begun parallel and left alone, can never touch.

In many ways the problem here has to do with a great deal more than race. There are millions of white Annas. But they make up a much smaller percentage of America's white population than is the case with the black poor. The white Annas do not define white America's image. Racism was literally postulated as a belief system to justify slavery, which in turn deconstructed families, languages, cultures, and the general social health of the black race, while spawning a vast new impoverished class of people at the end of the Civil War roughly coterminous with the entire community of blacks in America.

I have three children. My daughter Anike, a graduate of Spelman College, became a high school teacher in the Washington area. She is a gifted artist and poet whose submission won first prize in a national poetry contest. My son Jabari, who was a dean's list student at Howard, decided on law school. My daughter Khalea, who began attending Beauvoir, a private school in Washington, D.C., at age four, was reading somewhere above the sixth-grade level when she was in the third grade. (The reading proficiency tests administered to her age group measure only to the sixth grade.) On national standardized tests, she has scored in every tested area in the ninety-ninth percentile. I tell this not to brag, though I am vastly proud, but to make a point.

The state of Maryland has twenty-four counties. Every year the state administers to its public school students reading, writing, language usage, math, science, and social studies tests. Blacks in Maryland are concentrated in Prince Georges County and the City of Baltimore. In 1998, these two counties placed twenty-third and twenty-fourth in the test score standings.

These two predominately black counties did not score *behind* the predominately white counties because they are black any more than Khalea scored *ahead* of whites because she is black. Blacks scored behind in the two counties because of slavery's lasting legacy to them. Khalea scored ahead of the vast majority of whites because of the stimulating intellectual environment of her home generally and, more specifically, because her mother taught her the rudiments of reading before she had set foot in kindergarten. Khalea is an exception, and there are perhaps tens, if not hundreds, of thousands of blacks like her across the country. In broad terms, however, given the history of America's treatment of blacks, it is unsurprising that there are not more.

In this general discussion of academic achievement, the meaning of race is a subtle matter. Race is and is not the problem. Certainly rac*ism* caused the gap we see now. The discriminatory attitudes spawned to justify slavery ultimately guaranteed that, even after emancipation, blacks would be concentrated at the bottom of American society indefinitely. Blacks like Anna are not at the bottom because they are black individually but rather because of what they and their forebears have collectively had to endure because they were black. This important distinction, however, appears to be lost on many contemporary commentators who, being content to cite black failure without examining the causes, do more harm than good.

In a fall 1998 *New York Times* interview about gaps in academic achievement between genders and races in American society, Diane Ravitch, a senior fellow at the Brookings Institution, said: "They're saying that more girls take biology and chemistry, but uh-oh, there's more boys in physics. . . . This is not an alarm bell ringing in the night. What we should be concerned about is the racial disparities. There's a four-year gap between blacks and whites on national tests. The average black seventeen-year-old scores the same as the average thirteen-year-old. That's a crisis, not gender."

A little learning is, as they say, a dangerous thing, and particularly when it is presented, like a severely cropped photograph, as an independent truth. And I do not believe, as a general matter, that such truncated analyses are innocently delivered by white establishment academics.

After all, is race (a blinding buzz rubic) the most informative way, taken alone, to present relative performance achievement anyhow? If short people had been enslaved, reviled, kept illiterate, wrenched from their parents, sold off, raped, tortured, segregated, and denied equal access to the fruits of this country, would not the differences between short and taller people be just as great? In considering differences in current academic results, without considering the original cause to which I have referred, would not economic class divisions tell us more—not just about test gaps but about the very notion of race and its mystifying power to distort perceptions?

Yes, racism was used as a basis for justifying the hugely profitable enterprise of slavery. It was used during slavery and since to protect whites from having to accept responsibility for the bitter social harvest that we all live with today. Even now its myriad viruses deploy to project one group's history and obscure another's, to celebrate one people and disparage another, to advance a majority and hold back a minority. Must also the very ascientific social notion of race be allowed to strengthen its destructive properties, like a hurricane over water, before settling into the dangerously oversimplified language of conventional academic researchers?

How much can we learn from the writing of a social scientist who would compare an "average black student" to an "average white student"? No such people exist. Wouldn't it be a great deal more instructive to do achievement counterpart groupings while looking at the economic and social class environments that give rise to blacks and whites of relatively equal academic achievement? The data will tell us that the use of *race* by itself as a general category for comparison is a dangerously misleading decoy and no predictor of performance.

It would be fair to compare my daughter Khalea to the highest achievers in schools like hers where the annual tuition is $15,000 and virtually every parent has both an advanced college degree and the luxury of spending large blocks of time in the school, days or evenings; where six-year-olds meet Supreme Court justices during the school day and powerful accomplished figures at home; where Japanese, ballet, and drama are offered in after-school programs; where serious books are dissected in book clubs by serious nine-year-olds; where five-year-olds depart in the morning from nurturing home learning environments to travel by car to similarly stimulating environments at school. It would be fair, indeed, to compare Khalea to the top students (a group comprising blacks and whites) at her school and schools like hers. She has competed there very favorably. But her success is explained by her socioeconomic profile, not by her race.

Give a black or white child the tools (nurture, nutrition, material necessities, a home/school milieu of intellectual stimulation, high expectation, pride of self) that a child needs to learn and the child *will* learn. Race, at least in this regard, is irrelevant.

It would not be fair, then, to compare Khalea and those who attend her school to Sarah. Sarah was failing. She was failing when she should not have been. Again, race is not directly relevant. Sarah was not failing because she was black. She was failing for the same reasons that Appalachian white children fail. Grinding, disabling poverty. Unfortunately, blacks are heavily overrepresented among the ranks of America's desperately poor. Owing to race and only race, it was American slavery that created this bottom-rung disproportion, consigning *en masse* a whole people to unending penury and social debilitation.

It is obvious that in any effort to balance America's racial scales, education, defined in the broadest sense, must be assigned the very highest priority. Sadly, the very idea of public education, perhaps the most important load-bearing pillar of our society's future, has been under assault for decades. Even the segregated schools of my Richmond, Virginia, childhood were safer and had healthier academic environments than many public schools operating today—particularly those in deteriorating urban centers where public school populations are made up increasingly of children who are both black and poor.

Decades ago, the leaky public school ship began to list to starboard. Families of means (whites and relatively fewer blacks) occupying the upper-deck cabins nearest the ship's life-boats began evacuating the damaged craft in droves. A low panic energized the retreat as families, absent any unifying national leadership, came to believe that it was an every-family-for-itself situation. Although the vast majority of the country's families were still on board, trapped belowdecks, the country's leaders and well-to-do took markedly less interest in the plight of the trapped families after evacuees' children had reached safe haven on a veritable flotilla of sleek and exclusive new private school craft whose captains (for a tidy price) had virtually guaranteed to their young passengers a safe passage to the nation's very best colleges and universities. Meanwhile, the public school ship lay aground in shallows on its holed bottom going nowhere fast.

Much discussion ensued over what to do about the rusting

eyesore stuck drunkenly in five feet of silt. Liberals thought the ship could be raised with a great infusion of public resources and the re-enrollment of their children. The latter condition gave them pause. Conservatives were prepared, in effect, to let the doomed ship take "its own course."

4

SELF-HATRED

The greatest stumbling block in the way of progress in the race has invariably come from within the race itself. The monkey wrench of destruction as thrown into the cog of Negro Progress, is not thrown so much by the outsider as by the very fellow who is in our fold, and who should be the first to grease the wheel of progress rather than seeking to impede it.

—Marcus Garvey

L ET'S LANCE THE BOIL. We now hate ourselves. Not all of us, of course, but too many. Most of the rest of us have leaden doubts about our worth.

RURAL TEXANS MOURN DOGS KILLED BY TAINTED FOOD. The thousand-word *Washington Post* story about the death of thirty dogs appears above the fold on page three.

Explosions and fires from a broken gasoline pipeline in Nigeria have claimed the lives of over 1,000 Nigerians, burning most beyond recognition. The small story runs in the *New York Times* at the bottom of page six.

We don't know what has happened to us and no one will tell us. Thus we have concluded that the fault must be ours. We blame and disparage ourselves but seldom those responsible for our dilemma.

Surveys show that black South Africans prefer white immigrants, viewing new arrivals from Europe and North America more favorably than they do Africans. The story makes the front page of the *New York Times*.

At a Kennedy Center salute to black comedian Richard Pryor, Damon Wayans, who also is black, said to an overwhelmingly white audience that Mr. Pryor, while in Africa, had cause to fear that he might be cooked in a pot and eaten. The audience, at first bemused, quickly warmed to Mr. Wayans's brand of humor. Another black comedian, Chris Rock, joined with Mr. Wayans in the liberal use of the word "nigger" during his tribute to Mr. Pryor. Mercifully, these aspects of the story were not carried in the *New York Times* account. My wife and I endured them live.

What accounts for such self-degradation?

The answer lies in the past. As I said earlier, most African Americans have no knowledge of the history of our people before slavery or even that there exist richly detailed accounts of great African civilizations reaching back three thousand years and beyond. Most of us might not dare believe that a French nobleman and adventurer, Count Constantin de Volney, made the following observation in 1787:

> How we are astonished . . . when we reflect that to the race of Negroes, at present our slaves, and the objects of our extreme contempt, we owe our arts, sciences, and even the very use of speech, and when we recollect that, in the midst of those nations who call themselves the friends of liberty and humanity, the most barbarous of slaveries is justified; and that it is even a problem whether the understanding of Negroes be of the same species with that of white men.

Four years later, in his most famous work, *The Ruins: or a Survey of the Revolution of Empires*, Volney wrote that civilization had been first conceived "on the borders of the Upper Nile, among a black race of men."

That such views were commonly held before Volney's time

surprises many—and is a measure of slavery's comprehensive psychic and social costs, to those who bore them directly and to us their damaged descendants who bear them still today.

The screen adaptation of Toni Morrison's heroic novel *Beloved*, if not one the best movies ever, is far and away the most compelling and wrenching depiction of slavery yet brought to the American screen. When the film was screened before a largely black audience at the Union Station Cinema in Washington, D.C., viewers laughed at painful scenes brilliantly crafted to illustrate the mind-breaking psychological price of slavery's unbearable weight. At Washington's Fox Television News, a black film reviewer similarly mistook the film for a comedy.

Broadly ignorant of Africa's long and distinguished history previous to slavery, blacks and whites in America know of no era in which blacks were world innovators in the sciences and humanities. Blacks and whites are left to believe that we have always been behind. It is all that Hegel had hoped for. Thus the devastating, mutually reinforcing dual consequence: a pervasive global belief that blacks are inherently inferior and a crushing loss of confidence among blacks themselves. There follows a downward spiral to self-hate and the saddening spectacle of public black self-disparagement and, finally, an unparticularized miasma of anger.

The underlying premise cannot be overstated. In every competitive society, instruction in history and the humanities is a valuable instrument with which the dominant group, consciously or unconsciously, attempts to sustain its primacy, ill gotten or not. In America, whites control virtually every mainstream purveyor of instruction, academic and ephemeral. And in America, whites have caused all Americans to read, see, hear, learn and select from a diet of their own ideas, with few others placed to make suggestions, not to mention decisions. The airways, mainstream press, publishing houses, commercial distribution networks, school systems, universities and colleges, in one way or another are all controlled by whites. The museums are overwhelmingly established to celebrate white achievement. So are monuments, renamed rivers, mountains, valleys, dams, bridges, and streams. State and federal budgets, to which Asians, Hispanics, and African Americans contribute, are uniformly controlled by whites who seem to uniformly believe that the only ancestor worship worth funding is theirs.

Such thoughts will appear querulous only to the blinkered who've been reliably trained to resist thinking beyond the sills of their psychic needs. For the rest of us, the price of our inability to place ourselves in the fullness of world history has been crippling.

Of course these are all remediable injustices. In the search for answers, a simple change of heart, a fair awarding of resources, and a commitment to persevere would contribute nicely toward meeting the problem head on.

But there is little to encourage confidence that any of this will happen. Racist behavior in our society is largely static, unnoticed, unremarked, and unconsciously accommodated by Americans of all colors. Everyone essentially behaves as everyone always has. Habit dulls all senses, even the victim's, especially when the victim sees that crimes against the voiceless do not count.

———

The Cleveland Indians baseball team is composed of whites, blacks, and Hispanics. It is a distinguished and storied organization quartered at Jacobs Field, a state-of-the-art facility in downtown Cleveland. It had on its roster black and Hispanic players long before many other major league teams elected to bow to change. Larry Doby, Luke Easter, Mike Garcia, and a host of other blacks and Hispanics played for this, my favorite American League team, during the years of my childhood.

During the recent playoff series with the New York Yankees, I focused on Cleveland's David Justice, one of the club's black superstars. I wondered if he or any of his teammates had ever given any thought to their team's name. If any had, I'd never gotten wind of it.

But it wasn't the name that I'd thought about as I focused on Justice. It was the cap, or rather the logo that was stitched to it. The grin was hideous. The huge teeth hung from the roof of the head like gleaming convex stalactites that descended from the middle of the crown down to the cap's brim. The cavernous mouth crowded the nose and eyes into the hairline and strained without success to close around incisors that claimed three quarters of the clownish face. Had the face been black or brown, it would have incited urban riots, so patent was its insult. But the face was red and Justice wore the cap with jaunty insouciance.

The team had used the logo for years and not just on its caps. The grinning visage had graced everything from apparel to television promos. I would often find myself watching players talking to each other in the dugout as the monstrous teeth addressed each other from atop the players' oblivious heads.

I waited.

On ESPN, Fox, CNN, NBC, ABC, and CBS, the teeth would appear on the screen as large as the head of the sportscaster seated a safe distance in front of them.

I waited.

Following the lead of *USA Today*, the *New York Times* broke new ground and began to display the teeth in color on its sports pages.

I waited.

Not to be outdone, the Atlanta Braves began handing out replicas of their tomahawk symbol to fans at the ballpark, who would chant Indian-style with Jane Fonda, wife of the team's owner, while wielding the tomahawk in a murderous arc—fifty thousand partisans wailing in mindless concert. *Ay ya ya wa wa. Chop. Chop. Ay ya ya wa wa. Chop. Chop.*

I watched transfixed, and waited.

As a child growing up in Virginia during the 1940s and 1950s, I had watched the Washington Redskins, the only team we could follow, on the only channel we had, WTVR, Channel 6, the south's first television station (or so it described itself). George Preston Marshall, the Redskins' owner, hated blacks and would have none on his team. Marshall likely hated all colors of people save his own, and demonstrated his penchant for irony by emblazoning on his helmets the face of a race he probably disliked as much as mine. I'd like to claim that I had reasoned as a child that Marshall kept blacks off his teams because he feared that black players would find objectionable the Redskins' name and logo. I can't. Truth is, I hadn't given it any thought at all. In any case, Marshall needn't have been concerned. No Redskin player, black or white, has ever winced. Not even when the team made a mascot of a middle-aged black man who, dressed in the regalia of an indeterminate Native American tribe, whooped along the sidelines skinning teeth near the size of the Cleveland Indians'.

I waited.

I am a big sports fan and played basketball reasonably well in college. But through the years my spectatorship has largely been conducted via television. On occasion, between plays, I have allowed myself to imagine certain franchise transmutations. I would change the team's name and logo, and then try to gauge public reaction.

The Washington Redskins would become the Washington Blackskins. The logo on the helmet would look like the old caricatured Aunt Jemima. That Sunday, the Blackskins would be playing in Atlanta against Ted Turner's renamed football team, the Atlanta Mafia, who were coached by an Irishman named Maloney but known to all America variously as the Don and the Assassin. On the side of their helmets was a likeness of Al Capone. Before the game, toy machine guns had been handed to the Turner Field faithful, who screamed throughout on cue from Miss Fonda: *Rat tat tat. Rat tat tat. Thatsa deada Blackskin. Thatsa deada Blackskin.*

That same Sunday the New York Jews had a bye and did not play. One nationally syndicated sports columnist had written that the Jews did not play because they had had a "buy." No one seemed to notice. After all, it was all in good fun.

Across town at George Armstrong Custer Stadium, the New York Genocidists were wrapping up a four-game World Series sweep of the Massachusetts Pilgrim Feeders. The Indians had lost the first three games by large margins. The Genocidists, who wore blue and yellow uniforms reminiscent of the old U.S. horse cavalry, were led by a coach who called himself the General. The team's logo was a half-tone of a slightly inebriated Ulysses S. Grant. That evening, when the eleven-to-one score was announced on the evening news, the New York announcer said, "The Genocidists have slaughtered the Pilgrim Feeders once again."

Ay ya ya wa wa. Chop. Chop. Ay ya ya wa wa. Chop. Chop.

I go to some length here embroidering on racism expressed against Native Americans for a reason. As inclined as blacks understandably are by painful experience to believe the contrary, racism is not black-specific. It is like the Hydra, the lethal many-headed mythological snake whose heads regenerated as fast as they were severed. Racism is a social disease that exempts no race from either of its two rosters: victims and victimizers.

Don Rickles, the Jewish comedian, in a late-night television appearance on July 19, 1999, told host David Letterman that were it not for Mexicans, his bed would never be made at his Las Vegas hotel. It was a nakedly racist remark. Mr. Letterman took no notice. The audience chuckled. In making the remark, Mr. Rickles cast a vote not just for racism toward Mexicans, but for religious, ethnic, and racial intolerance toward blacks, Asians, gentiles and Jews as well. For the varieties of bigotry spring from a common root. To tolerate one form, either wittingly or not, is to accept all the rest. In order to contain the disease, and not just its various expressions, the contagion must be attacked at its root, and with the full, undiluted force of the *whole* of society. A slur against any group by a member of another can never go unremarked if our society is to have any long-term future.

And then, of course, for African Americans there is a particular relevance in all this. While African Americans have won from America scarcely a fraction of their due, they have at least achieved a measure of recognition as victims of racism. Native Americans have yet to become so broadly noticed as contemporary victims, apparently not even by many African Americans. For the reasons I have given, this weakens the cause not only of Native Americans but of all other victimized Americans as well, African Americans prominently included.

To be sure, the Native Americans themselves have long protested the dehumanizing use of their likenesses and cultural nomenclature as fodder for team sports emblems. But no one else much seems to care. It's as if, no matter the injury, no matter the pain, a wrong is a wrong only when acknowledged in the broad mainstream of our society. When the victims are small in number, peripheral and voiceless, woe be unto them, even when the hurt is completely gratuitous, contributes to costly social disintegration, and lengthens the distance between us as Americans.

I must confess that as I write the whole of this I feel a despair that, in their ignored state, Native Americans must certainly feel. I, as they do, fully expect to be ignored by the larger society which, perhaps as a measure of simple guilt avoidance, appears invariably inclined against any exploration of the *causes* of our nation's complex racial and social problems. It may be this particular never-disappointed expectation that summons involuntarily the slave-era lyric that plays in my head now over and over again:

> *O, I couldn't hear nobody pray,*
> *O Lord, I couldn't hear nobody pray,*
> *O, way down yonder by myself,*
> *And I couldn't hear nobody pray,*
> *On ma knees, wid ma burden,*
> *Couldn't hear nobody pray.*

Pain is difficult. Unremarked, unacknowledged, unobserved pain is usually lethal to collective psychic health. Social harmony, at the least, is an early sure victim.

In response to my memoir, I received what amounts to the

same letter from twenty or so white Americans—self-described earnest liberals from whom blacks had commanded attention by assaulting them. One such victim wrote:

> I will flat out tell you, there is much hatred and ill will towards the blacks, but not because of the color of their skin—it is behavior, behavior, behavior. The blacks have behavioral standards so low, everyone hates them and mistrusts them.

Whether so or not, it had certainly been the writer's conviction. But if so, why such behavior? Causes? He had not looked for any beyond the threshold of his own short-lived inconvenience. He had drawn no line backward in time. He assumed no condition of the past, near or far, to be formative of his assailant—or of him. The world had begun in the morning and had no derivation. His crudely benign blindness was a metaphor of America's. *Everyone hates them and mistrusts them.* The cause had become the effect.

In the Islamic world the camera is often seen as an accursed contraption that steals the soul and violates its spirit. Slavery is my camera. Down the sides of its broad ugly mass drape the inky shadows that block the whole of memory and bedevil still the coreless self.

————

When I was a little boy growing up in a gray downtown flat with space heaters, the only white man I saw to speak to, apart from the Jewish grocers for whom I worked, was a Willy Loman-like character who collected insurance premiums for the Richmond Beneficial Life Insurance Company. I liken him to Arthur Miller's character in *Death of a Salesman* in retrospect, of course. He seemed to me anything but that in the late 1940s and early 1950s.

He came to our door once a month, although I can picture the physical appearance of the man only in the warmest stretch of summer. I think he must have been in his early fifties. I can't be sure because the camera eye of a child tends to add years, in much the same way that the eye of the middle-aged wants badly to subtract them. I do remember clearly, though, that he seemed always to be out of breath as he crossed our bowed plank porch to rap on the hooked screen door. The screen was dirty and ballooned outward toward the agent, almost touching his nose as he spoke. Mama had, without success, tried to stop her four children from opening the screen door by pushing against the screen itself. Eventually the metal mesh would dislodge from its wooden frame and present a small hazard around its jagged edges, although I am reasonably certain that the hazard was not covered by our policy.

"Good mowning, Miz Robinson." The agent had a generous smile that reddened his ample cheeks and pushed up the corners of his eyes. He wore a single-breasted seersucker suit that was dampened by perspiration running in trickles down into his curling shirt collar. I remember the suit so clearly because I had been obliged at one point to wear my brother Max's hand-me-down seersucker suit. The funny-feeling fabric seemed to have no talent for holding its form.

"How are you today?" Mama responded.

"I'm fine and how are the little ones?"

"Everyone's fine, thank you."

Mama pushed the screen door open and handed four one-dollar bills to the agent. The premium was $3.56 a month or

89 cents a week on a policy that would pay $2,000 upon my father's death.

"I got your change right here." The agent retrieved from his pocket forty-four cents and counted the coins out to Mama. "Awful hot today," the agent said as he wiped his neck with a soggy handkerchief.

And so it went for years.

I seem to remember that we liked the man although we knew nothing of him beyond what we could see through our impaired screen door for a few seconds a month. He was polite. He smiled. He was the nicest white person we knew anything about in Richmond, Virginia, during the early 1950s. He might well have been a rabid segregationist, a Klan grand wizard, or a Stonewall Jackson fan club organizer. We didn't explore such possibilities. It was enough that he was civil. It didn't turn him into Mahatma Gandhi but it raised him by our measure above the plane of most white folks. His smile actually provoked in my child's breast something close to gratitude. I should have been embarrassed by this insight, but I was not.

I was sick, you see—suffering from some form of nonspecific rejection disorder, a derivative perhaps of Stockholm syndrome, or good-cop-bad-cop, whatever. We had been treated like subhumans. More had been done to us, more had been taken from us, than we could consciously reckon. The agent, who lived far across town in a neighborhood I had never seen, smiled at us. And we liked him for it. It was as simple as that. Or so I thought at the time.

———

In May 1999 my wife, my daughters, Khalea and Anike, and I attended the graduation of my son, Jabari, at Howard University's Burr Gymnasium. The commencement was one of several smaller commencements held before the large all-inclusive exercise.

Burr Gymnasium had about it the festive, proud feel that all commencements have. Every seat was filled with parents, grandparents, children, friends, dressed in the gay pastels of spring. The air conditioning barely kept pace, and I understood for the first time the long pre-Freon tradition of holding commencements out of doors. Program bulletins had been converted to hand fans and fluttered like butterflies around the tiered seats that encircled the gymnasium's floor where the robed graduating seniors sat expectantly below. Howard held these subcommencements so that each graduate—or, just as important, each graduate's parents—would get to hear his or her name called before receiving the long-sought college diploma.

I like commencements, although I never participated in a single one of my own (high school, college, law school). I like them still. And I especially like those at historically black institutions, for they are stories of bright black promise that answer full enough on sunny warm mornings the gloomy surveys of our world's social condition. Black families go to commencements with a unique vigor. Mothers and fathers embrace their children in the exuberant aftermaths, exhaust rolls of film, float with pride. A 4.0-grade-point summa cum laude graduate is announced and the audience says with its sustained applause that the student has done something wonderful.

I looked at my son, as no doubt the other parents looked at their children, nearly unwaveringly for the duration of the two-hour program. Then the larger, graver reality I have been discussing was brought back to me when an exemplary young woman gave the farewell to the class of 1999.

"If I were French I would say *merci*, if I were German I would say *danke schoen*, if I were Italian I would say *grazie* . . . but I will simply say thank you." My wife and I looked at each other, both thinking the young woman's remarks revealingly odd, both suspecting that few others in the assemblage shared our dismay. The young woman was indeed not French or German or Italian. She was not a European American of any variety. She was an American of *African* descent. Why on earth was she iffing herself European?

Some will read this and think my reaction overblown. In fact, what the young woman had said was a very normal thing. And practically everyone there took it as such.

But what if she had been a white woman graduating from the University of Oklahoma? What if she had said to a largely white sea of fellow graduates, family members, and friends: "If I were Tanzanian, I would say *kwaheri*, if I were Malawian, I would say *tsalani bwino*, if I were Senegalese, I would say *djam ak djam* . . ."? I think you get the drift here. Not just one lone couple would have looked at each other, puzzled. Virtually everybody would have been, to say the least, dumbfounded.

Not so in the black community. And it is the very normalcy of our self-denial, our self-ignorance, that is so troubling. It all leads me to wonder whether any group of people in the world has been more resolutely, if unconsciously, committed to notions of self-abnegation than blacks. Well-trained, quiet-flowing, oblivious, uncritical, near total cultural self-abnegation. It is akin to driving in heavy night fog. Little can be seen of where we're going, less still of where we've been. The thickness of the blanket pitch steals our confidence. We conclude that the only hope is to follow the broken white line that snakes in the darkness.

5

DEMANDING RESPECT

Power never concedes anything without a demand. It never has and it never will.

—Frederick Douglass

I N AUGUST of 1998 polls revealed that 94 percent of black Americans approved of the way President Bill Clinton was handling his job, 34 percentage points higher than the job performance rating of 60 percent given to the president by white Americans. When Clinton was elected to his first term in 1992, he received 83 percent of the black vote compared to 39 percent of the white vote. In the 1996 election for a second term, Clinton received 84 percent of the black vote compared to 43 percent from whites.

In a 1997 poll, the Joint Center for Political and Economic Studies found President Clinton to be more popular among African Americans than either the Reverend Jesse Jackson or General Colin Powell, the former chairman of the Joint Chiefs of Staff.

I was puzzled by this until I remembered my childhood feelings toward the Richmond Beneficial Life Insurance agent.

"What he has been able to project, unlike any other president in recent memory, is that he is completely comfortable with black Americans," said theater producer George C. Wolfe.

The Reverend Joseph E. Lowery, former president of the

Southern Christian Leadership Conference, said, and I cannot know if altogether seriously, "It's the saxophone, the man has soul."

To the rejection disorder, perhaps I should invite a look at its corollary, the Pied Piper syndrome.

All of this black support had either to cynically amuse Bill Clinton or to greatly befuddle him. I could all but read his thoughts: *Why do they love me so? What have I done?* Beyond cabinet and other job appointments that have small impact on the general black community, Bill Clinton did discernibly little for black people.

In his first term, Clinton's policies followed a distinct slant toward a more conservative and Republican course on social issues. He sponsored the most punitive crime bill in history, which passed in 1993; after suffering the defeat of his "economic stimulus package," which contained funds for urban development, he never put it back on the table. He signed the most punitive welfare reform bill in history, effecting a revolution in New Deal policy toward government support for the poor; and thousands of people silently have been sifted out of federal government employment through the "reinventing government program."

Clinton, however, has maintained his grip on black voters by praying with them in black churches, touting a "mend it, don't end it" affirmative action plan, appointing the largest number of blacks to government positions, and paying more attention to Africa than any previous president. Yet, when one examines the impact of the crime bill on the sharply increased criminalization of black youth in particular, the exposure of the poorest blacks to the labor market without sufficient training or family support, and the lack of investment in urban schools or communities, Clinton's positive initiatives may be viewed as largely symbolic.
—Ronald Walters

This should not surprise. No segment of the national electorate has given more but demanded and received less from the Democratic Party nationally than African Americans. We don't take ourselves seriously, therefore no one else does. Our support can be won with gestures. *No* quid pro quo is required.

How could President Clinton help but ruminate, *I can't understand the blacks. There is no apparent reason for their support of me, except that I am not a Republican, which for them appears to be reason enough.*

By 1999 at least seventeen states were doing business with twenty for-profit private prison companies that bring in annually more than a quarter of a billion dollars in revenues from taxpayer dollars. These private prisons are unlicenced and unregulated. They are proliferating rapidly for reasons that are straightforward. Profits are high. Costs associated with safety and accountability have been slashed to the bone. Few of the new facilities offer the work-training and education programs that have been shown to reduce recidivism. Cruel and inhumane prison environments are being jerry-built—for profit and without public accountability—to warehouse those who will ultimately return to society with a greater potential for menace than before being locked up.

For its part, the Clinton administration contributed to the disproportionate incarceration of blacks by refusing to support equalized sentencing for the sale and possession of crack and powder cocaine. Crack is largely the drug choice of poor blacks, powder cocaine the choice for financially better-off whites. Jail terms for crack sales and possession are illogically longer than they are for powder cocaine. Ergo, blacks, being more likely to be imprisoned than whites and imprisoned

longer, for what in essence is the same offense, are now disproportionately more likely to be held in the growing white-
owned for-profit unregulated private hells.

I am no clairvoyant, but Clinton's thoughts are legible
enough to me: *Maybe the blacks just don't know about this stuff, but
how could they not?*

In the state of Washington, blacks make up less than 4 percent of the state's population but make up almost 40 percent
of the state's prison population. Although blacks account for
only 2.8 percent of undergraduates at the University of Washington (the only public university in the state said to have used
affirmative action in admissions), Washingtonians overwhelmingly approved in November 1998 a resolution banning "preferential treatment" based on race or sex to any group in the
public sector. This placed the state in a group with California
(which had earlier approved a similar resolution) and three
other states (Texas, Louisiana, and Mississippi) that had sought
and won through the courts bans against preferential treatment
in university admissions. Such actions underscored a disturbing
general decline, roughly coinciding with President Clinton's
tenure, in national black college enrollment.

Meanwhile, President Clinton's much ballyhooed advisory
board on race relations ended fifteen months of work with a
modest report that called for little more than another panel.
Reacting to the board's recommendations, Harvard law professor Randall Kennedy (hardly a screed hurler) said, "Those
sound like a list of platitudes. My goodness, there is nothing
substantive there. It's not like I'm searching for a fight, but
that's not exactly giving people direction. Talk about lowest
common denominator."

The black leaders almost never place upon me specific demands, and even when they do, they seldom follow through. But still, the blacks saved our Democratic cookies in the fall of '98.

It can be argued that in the conduct of domestic policy President Clinton has had to compromise with a Republican congress that has plainly shown itself to be more hostile than he to the black community's interests. In the area of foreign affairs, however, where the President has enjoyed relatively unfettered latitude, he can hardly shelter from criticism by pleading the constraints of compromise.

Item: At least four friendly Caribbean democracies—St. Lucia, Dominica, St. Vincent, and Grenada—may collapse because of Clinton's efforts to transfer European markets for Caribbean bananas to Chiquita Brands' Carl H. Lindner, a Lincoln Bedroom alumnus and large campaign contributor. Clinton threatened to impose 100 percent tariffs on European wine, cheese, and other exports unless the Europeans cease reserving a small slice of their markets for their former colonies in the Caribbean, Africa, and the Pacific. In imperiling the economy of the four tiny Caribbean democracies, Clinton has made them more vulnerable to drug trafficking, although the U.S. exports no bananas and no U.S. jobs are at stake.

Item: Charging that a Sudanese facility had produced chemical weapons for Osama bin Laden, the United States bombed a pharmaceutical factory in Khartoum, the capital of Sudan, killing an indeterminate number of people. The Sudanese government called upon President Clinton to produce evidence that the factory had produced anything other than pharmaceuticals. The president was unable to do so. Within days of the attack, people, some in our own government, wondered aloud if flawed intelligence had led the president to blow up the wrong site. No one I spoke to could imagine him even considering bombing a building (even with proof of chemical weapons production) in a western European capital.

Item: In 1994 President Clinton avoided steps that might have curbed the Rwanda genocide which resulted in the deaths of 500,000 Tutsis at the hands of Hutus. Writing about the withdrawal from Rwanda of a United Nations peacekeeping force, Philip Gourevitch in *We Wish to Inform You That Tomorrow We Will Be Killed with Our Families* laments, "The desertion of Rwanda by the UN force was Hutu power's greatest diplomatic victory to date, and it can be credited almost single-handedly to the United States. . . . Madeleine Albright [U.S. ambassador to the United Nations at the time] . . . is rarely associated with Rwanda, but ducking and pressuring others to duck, as the death toll leapt from thousands to tens of thousands to hundreds of thousands, was the absolute low point in her career as a stateswoman."

The black people love me. I don't really know why, but all they seem to care about are the symbolic things like cabinet appointments.

The late Ronald H. Brown, secretary of commerce in Clinton's first cabinet, and Mike Espy, Clinton's first secretary of agriculture, both blacks, were required to submit urine samples for drug testing before joining the cabinet. At least two white members of the cabinet, Interior Secretary Bruce Babbitt and Carol E. Browner, head of the Environmental Protection Agency, have said that no such requirement was made of them.

You won't believe this, but for the black voters' turnout in the fall '98 congressional elections, the blacks required of us absolutely nothing. Can you believe that?

The purpose here is not to lacerate Bill Clinton, or even to urge blacks to withdraw support from the Democratic Party. A temporary sobering comeuppance, however, would do wonders for us and the Democrats. We have lavished unconditional support perennially upon Democratic office seekers and gotten for it what one invariably gets for unconditional support: nothing.

Silly us. Or, at least, silly *outsider* us. The *insider* us—black elected Democrats, black appointed Democrats, selected black entrepreneurs—well now, this assemblage has received something for its trouble, ranging from the significant (government friendliness for private wealth-building) to a job or just plain, banal blandishment (a seat on the president's plane to Africa).

In 1999 the House Republicans discovered themselves game for this cynical competition for black affections, outflanking their Democratic colleagues by electing their own pliable black to a House Republican leadership post. The House black leadership score just after the they-saved-our-cookies fall 1998 elections: Republicans—J. C. Watts; Democrats—zero.

Though we may be vulnerable to gestures, it is difficult to believe that Republicans are dim-witted enough to think that such microtokens will draw blacks en masse into a party that opposes not only affirmative action but federal support for such minimally salutary notions as nutrition standards for school meals, meat inspection measures to protect us from E. coli and other deadly microbes, Medicaid, Medicare, clean air, clean water, a livable minimum wage, and (may the saints protect us in Salem) contraception. But then, Republican optimism about gaining black support may be driven by the loopy inexplicable logic of our lopsidedly disproportionate ardor for Clinton. Inasmuch as the intensity of our support made no rational sense whatsoever, Republicans may just as loopily deduce that a rightward surge could be in the offing for us.

But, for the *outsider* us, if the income gap remains intractably yawning, if black college enrollment is in fact dropping, if blacks remain overrepresented in prison, on death row, in unemployment lines, in homeless shelters, on assorted bar charts of misery indices, well then, does our party loyalty matter? The documented truth of our continued laggardness renders all of the close-order debate among the president, Democrats, Republicans, and black leaders rather myopically beside the point, doesn't it? After all, the object here is to close all socioeconomic gaps between the races. The intramural tango of bitsy Democratic palliatives and itsy-bitsy Republican palliatives does little more than divert attention and siphon energy as a recondite rot steals up inexorably from the underside, narrowing our practical freedoms and troubling our tenous contentment.

I am trying here to think larger, beyond the needling, sapping, distracting details of a race debate wholly in the wrong place, but it is difficult to do this with any sureness and confidence, to find language for a discourse yet to be held. A tangle of nameless, nebulous thoughts clamor for description, while I struggle even to hear myself think in the face of the public career types with their heads vised in a thoroughly disproved orthodoxy, their voices claiming variety but in fact chiming in a tedium of pointless concert, their eyes all blinkered, their feet long set upon the easy path.

Truths that would suggest workable strategies lie about in the landscape. Truths pummeled to inertness by politicians. Camouflaged, hidden, decoyed, ignored, but truths nonetheless. Like matter, they can neither be destroyed nor invented. They simply lie there in the open awaiting regard.

Perhaps we should check first for consensus on a course setting before exploring strategies. I suspect that the better part of the predicament is that we lack a critical mass for identifying the problem we seek to solve.

I would state the objective this way:

There will always be differences in the abilities and achievements of individuals, but achievement differences that correlate with race must never be tolerated. That gap must be fully closed.

But how many share this objective? Clearly not everyone. Clearly not most. I would argue: not even most blacks. The endless gauntlet exacts its price in lowered expectation.

To do what is necessary, of course, will require a virtual Marshall Plan of federal resources, far in excess of anything contemplated between the nearly touching poles of conventional palliatives. But I see no evidence of any will to do anything much. In the areas of mathematics and reading, for example, a variety of pedagogical techniques have been developed that would work well enough if picked up and used broadly. No need to discuss them here. Their efficacy has been proved. That's not the problem. The problem is one of will—and consensus on course setting.

There is much new fessing-up that white society must be induced to do here for the common good. First, it must own up to slavery and acknowledge its debt to slavery's contemporary victims. It must, at long last, pay that debt in massive restitutions made to America's only involuntary members. It must help to rebuild the black esteem it destroyed, by democratizing access to a trove of histories, near and ancient, to which blacks contributed seminally and prominently. It must open wide a scholarly concourse to the African ancients to which its highly evolved culture owes much credit and gives none. It must rearrange the furniture of its national myths, monuments, lores, symbols, iconography, legends, and arts to reflect the contributions and sensibilities of all Americans. It must set afoot new values. It must purify memory. It must recast its lying face.

But none of this will happen, even as a recondite rot steals up exorably from the underside, narrowing our practical freedoms and troubling our tenous contentment. Unless . . .

Unless some critical number of *renaissance* blacks can wrench us away from the minced-step rusted strategic template to which our noses have been welded, can eschew politicians, black and white, as the self-limiting, self-protecting pragmatists they invariably if involuntarily are, and can dramatically comprehend and address the broad whole of the enormous psychic wrong done to us through the long ages, with American complicity. They must strike a spark from vestigial flints still buried deep in our embattled spirits. They must find our voice and implacably demand our whole due. They must propagate an intellectual storm of self-discovery among blacks tantamount to a secular religion. They must make us whole again where our secrets fester, so as not to squander our due. They must bring us to the table, confident, self-knowing, imbued with all the requisite values, equal in every measure save the material. For these are the things only we can do for ourselves. Until we do, no Marshall Plan for our material renovation can work. Until we do, no call for a broad American racial policy reconsideration will be heeded.

None of this is new. But perhaps the time can now be right as it never was before. God, I think often of how lonely and despairing Robeson and Du Bois must have felt, standing in a mainstream gale, killing-mean with the volatile mix of racism and anticommunism that mowed down all who dared question it. At a time when towering American men of letters like

Thomas Wolfe could write gratuitously, even casually, about a "homesick nigger" or "nigger junk" and raise hardly a hackle among their adoring white peers. When *The Birth of a Nation*, a praise song for the Ku Klux Klan, could win for its creator, D. W. Griffith, an Academy Award. When hooded night riders were "disappearing" blacks in America willy-nilly, long before the new verb would be suggested to our lexicon by the cruel acts of oligarchs in Central and South America.

Later, in the 1960s and early 1970s, a comparatively small number of blacks would try to arouse us from our leeward course, but by then black elites had chosen to see integration as a panacea for virtually all of our problems. Those who tried to warn that there could be more had little chance of being listened to. The elites had been included *in*, which gave them bigger voices, voices that were in any case toned, modulated, university-inflected, and hence more credible.

The alternative voices of dissent never touched the marrow of the black mainstream. For reasons that were never clear to me, they elected to set themselves apart from those they presumed to lead by dressing and talking differently, using an unfamiliar idiom and cadence, leaving their voices up at the end of their sentences in what sounds, in retrospect, to have been a forerunner of Valley-speak. They seemed deeply suspicious, often with good reason, of those blacks who had received from white institutions a liberal arts education, which I think they viewed as rather closer to indoctrination. They considered blacks who'd gone to places like Harvard Law School accommodationists, as indeed a good many of us were.

Looking back on it, the elites were right, but only partially so. The voices of dissent were every bit as right, but woefully bereft of tools. They have faded to quiet now. The black community badly needs their fire—combined with an element of erudition without which broad credibility is simply not achievable. Suffice it to say that black elected officials, alone, will lead the black community nowhere near where it needs to go. They will put us under no levitating sunlight, suggest no unplotted course, ask no new questions, and apprehend no need of undiscovered forebears whose truths for us are as old as time.

———

We had gone to dinner at Hamburger Hamlet, a midpriced restaurant appointed in faux Old English and staffed with friendly college-aged waiters. Hazel and Khalea and I had joined Joyce and Smithson Haughton at the restaurant the evening of their arrival in Washington on vacation from their home in St. Croix, U.S. Virgin Islands. Somewhat new friends, the Haughtons had been married for more than thirty years. They had about them the feel of a companionship that had matured like a memorable Bordeaux. They were diametrical opposites who, owing to that, found each other immensely amusing. He spoke with muted reticence, she with convicted assurance. She was witty and funny; he, without such gift, merrily beamed at hers. He was tall and rail thin. She was shortish and plump. When one spoke, the other listened. They finished each other's sentences. Their marriage spoke a language. It spoke it subtly, quietly, but unmistakably.

A male waiter brought our drinks and placed them on the heavy oak table.

"Pardon me," Smithson said to the waiter, "but would you bring us some coasters, please."

"I'm sorry, sir, but we don't have any."

———

"I'm sorry, but did you say you don't have any?"

"Yes—or no we don't."

They looked at each other as if mutually mystified. The waiter left. Smithson and Joyce then looked at each other briefly in a language I could not read.

Driving home, I would ask Hazel, "What was that about the coasters?"

"Caribbeans always put coasters under drinks. No one puts a glass down directly on a table."

Hazel and I had been together for sixteen years, much of it spent in the Caribbean, and I had never noticed.

Smithson had begun to talk at length of his passion for sailing, a passion that appeared to be shared by Joyce, if for no other reason than it was his and they came as a set, the giver and receiver in their union having long since dissolved to indistinguishable, interchangeable. He demonstrated a sailing maneuver with hands that were large with spatulate fingers that seemed made for the ropes.

Once, in Boca Raton, Hazel and I, with no knowledge of sailing, had chartered a long sloop to take us out for an afternoon on a choppy sea well beyond hailing distance. Our crew was a single sail-muscling fifty-nine-year-old whose medical chart we were not privy to. Had he had a coronary or slipped from the sloped wet deck into the sea, we'd as likely have ended up in Bora Bora as at our point of embarkation.

(Hazel and I have, I confess, a yen for moderate adventure. In late December 1988 we flew on a small propeller-driven craft in and out of the breathtaking canyons of the Hawaiian islands. I had sat beside Dave, the pilot, in the copilot's seat— although I know no more about flying than I do about sailing— as Dave aimed the plane at the canyon's jagged walls to afford us better camera angles. While we were threading our way, *blat-blat-blat*, through the canyons' narrow corridors, Hazel, from her bulkhead seat directly behind Dave, sought reassurance from the posted aircraft inspection certificate that was framed and displayed on the bulkhead wall. *There is none so blind as he who will not see.* The certificate was dated 1961.)

In any case, Smithson had held us for a lengthy spell in some measure of thrall with their tropical sailing stories, which served to symbolize the poetic logic of his and Joyce's long easy time together.

Over coffee, the evening having spent itself, the discussion deteriorated to Bill Clinton's troubles relating to Monica Lewinsky. Inasmuch as St. Croix is an American possession, the Haughtons, though they had spent their entire lives in the Caribbean, were American citizens. They were, at the same time, very much West Indians, with lilting accents learned on a lush island not far from Hazel's St. Kitts.

"I think what they're doing to Clinton is terrible." Joyce was referring to Clinton's treatment at the hands of Kenneth Starr and the roasting the president was getting in the general press. "I love Clinton," Joyce said. "I just love the man."

Hazel and I smiled but said nothing. We liked them very much. She had been fervid in her declaration. The silence that greeted it opened something of a hole in the dinner party's rhythm.

"Well, I take it that you don't share my view."

This is never easy. Especially when said to friends who mean well, who are decent people, who work hard and rear fine children and vote in every election. Illusions are comforting and probably essential to some degree for our contentment, if not our sanity.

"One problem is," Hazel said, "his attacks on the countries of the Caribbean. He's joining with Chiquita to wreck the economies of a lot of Caribbean countries." It was impossible to make it sound like anything other than a rebuke.

"What?" Joyce looked embarrassed.

I remembered stopping in Washington after my first year of law school to see my brother Max. We were joined in his home by a woman friend of his who wrote for *Newsweek* magazine. As the discussion turned to the presidential campaign of that year, I offered that the Republican Nelson Rockefeller seemed to me worthy enough of black support. The *Newsweek* writer asked me how much I really knew about Rockefeller and his policy attitudes toward blacks. The fact was, I knew almost nothing about Rockefeller and immediately felt foolish. Rockefeller had generally supported civil rights, had a nice smile, and was often seen pictured with blacks. This had been basis enough for my opinion. I developed a speedy and completely unwarranted dislike for my brother's writer friend.

And then, of course, there is the debilitating disease of vertical celebrity worship. By the late 1960s, Alabama's George Wallace had race-baited his way to national prominence, preaching a brand of white supremacy that heightened racial tensions throughout the South and indirectly resulted of the deaths of an indeterminate number of blacks. Wallace came to Boston during this time and stayed at a hotel where a black law school classmate's mother worked as a maid. Wallace, upon encountering my friend's mother in a hotel hallway, extended his hand and greeted her warmly. She took his hand and returned his greeting.

"Mama, how could you have? He hates black people."

She had told her son of the encounter with the famous governor with a measure of pride. Her reaction to Wallace was not surprising. I'd venture that most people are to some degree disabled in the presence of large celebrity. It addles the mind like temporary insanity and ought be studied with as much gravity.

No one's celebrity equals the president's and, not unlike his predecessors, Clinton has used it in his own interest by surrounding himself with people, black and white, who do not discomfort him appreciably with demands he would prefer not to address. The simple notion of husbanding political capital requires that he make as small a policy commitment to us as possible in exchange for our support. This, perforce, obliges an effort to transmogrify those of us near him into Indian scouts. Suffice it to say that, historically, the Oval Office has worked its enfeebling sorcery on a countless many (blacks and whites) who've entered with sturdy convictions and exited buckled at the knee and put off their course.

Ordinary citizens who view the president from a distance, of course, are able to see what he does and does not do *less* clearly. This is particularly the case when the "Indian scouts" tell them that all is well and sally forth to rally the vote. One can look at the recent example of Kenya to help point up the universality of this principle.

Princess Diana's and Monica Lewinsky's biographer, Andrew Morton, wrote a biography of Kenya's president, Daniel arap Moi, who has run his country with a corrupt and abusive band for more than twenty years. Mr. Moi, seventy-five, has held on to power by accommodating graft, opposing multiparty democracy, and fomenting ethnic tension. Still many Kenyans have seen their president as something of a cipher.

In the book, *Moi: The Making of an African Statesman*, Mr.

Morton writes: "Perhaps because serving his nation is now second nature, he rarely, if ever, thinks of himself before his country." Mr. Morton goes on to unconvincingly explain away the murder of a Moi rival, Foreign Minister Robert Ouko, whose death many Kenyans have linked to several close associates of the president. Many, if not most, Kenyans believe their president to be an exponent of Joseph Stalin's famous maxim "Where there is a man, there's a problem. No man, no problem." Still others know little of their leader. "Everyone wants to know the personal life of the President—about why he is such a great President and what his secret is being so powerful, great and energetic," commented bookshop owner Jitesh R. Upadhyay to the *New York Times*.

Of course, Clinton is not Moi, and Moi is not typical of Africa's leaders. All leaders, however, democratic or not, hide themselves from their constituents, so as to present the smallest possible political target. They usually do this through some alchemy of high-office aura and gilded half-truth to make good little deeds appear important and big bad deeds simply go away.

Joyce had ardently declared: "I love Clinton. I just love the man." Yet she knew almost nothing about what the president had actually done on a range of issues she would have been concerned about had she an inkling of the decisions Clinton was making or not making. I've come to believe from long experience that most Americans are like Joyce, just as I had been long ago in my uninformed approval of Nelson Rockefeller.

———

Maynard Jackson, when he was mayor of Atlanta, told me once that all African Americans should carry on their persons a laminated card listing the policies that would benefit our community. Whenever approached for support by a local, state, or national politician, the bearer would whip out the card and read it aloud to the candidate for office. The race of the candidate would not matter. All would have to face "the card." After all, this was business. The card would be blown up to poster size and posted in black churches, community assembly halls, barber shops, beauty parlors, restaurants, stores. It would be affixed to utility poles and streetlight stanchions. Black taxi drivers would display it in the plastic jackets holding their chauffeur's licenses against their dashboards.

A national database would be created to facilitate the dissemination of the wallet-size cards. Millions would be mailed to blacks in New York, Los Angeles, Philadelphia, and Chicago. Hundreds of thousands would be sent to St. Louis, Kansas City, Mobile, Dallas, Detroit, and Memphis, with enough available to cover the handful of blacks in Maine, Vermont, Montana, and the Dakotas. *Essence*, *Ebony*, *Black Enterprise*, and *Emerge* would run the card in their magazines four times a year as a public service.

A group of respected national black leaders would negotiate the language of the card's demands. No elected official would sit with this group, and it was not immediately clear how the group's size would be determined or its members chosen. What had been determined, and I think wisely, was that the card's demands would not exceed twenty, would include at least two or three foreign policy issues, and would frame the demands as concise questions requiring a simple yes or no for an answer. Fudging would be scored as failure by the grading black organizations, which would require anyone seeking an endorsement to submit to the *card test* before being allowed to address any meeting of its members. This would allow members to have the candidate's score in hand while sitting through speeches of dulcet self-promotion.

Test scores would be publicized. Instructions on the back of the card would oblige a bearer, as a matter of honor, to vote for the candidates who'd scored highest and against any who'd flunked. Although it was acknowledged that the card could not cover all of a given constituent's concerns, it would cover a basic menu of fundamental, baseline matters. Of course, the questions would not be static and would be revised as election cycles bore forward. It was also hoped that the card's success would inspire local versions with a more particularized relevance for local elections.

As it turned out, every black organization of any consequence endorsed the card idea and it became unimaginably successful, bearing benefits that had not been contemplated by those who had conceived the idea. Here are some examples of the card's unanticipated effect.

First, it appeared to reduce the value of candidate endorsements from famous blacks and famous people generally. Consider the case of Senator Ben N. Office, a strapping hail-fellow-well-met veteran of the U.S. Senate who could overbear you with the ruddy charm he had used to win the black vote in his state over the last three elections. On a Tuesday evening in October he had come to address a state association of black educators. Taking no chances, the senator swept into the conference hall wearing a beatific smile, accompanied by a vastly popular black champion prizefighter.

"Hiya, hiya. Good to see you again," the senator said to people he'd never before met, as he made his way toward the podium. Upon reaching the lectern, he boomed out to the educators, "The champ and I hope we can count on your support again."

"What about the card?" asked a chorus of voices.

"What card?" answered Senator Ben N. Office, suddenly unsure of himself.

"*This* card," said the champion boxer. "We need your answers to twenty questions. Yes or no, please."

The champ whipped out his card and began to read the questions to the flummoxed senator, who proceeded to fail the test, lose both the black vote and his office, and scare from his successor better policies than any the black community had ever seen from Office.

By the time Office left office, the cards had proliferated through the national black community like wildfire. Across the country, blacks formed hundreds if not thousands of study groups to flesh out their understanding of the important issues described on the card. Library patronage by blacks soared. On Sundays, blacks watching candidates on *Meet the Press* and *Face the Nation* consulted the candidates' card scores as they watched. Schoolchildren took to learning the questions as verse. Blacks began to account to each other as they required others to account to them because of the card. A new study undertaken by the Joint Center for Political Studies showed that the card had resulted in a 30 percent increase in black voting. A related study undertaken by the National Association of Black Psychologists revealed that the card was causing blacks to feel better about themselves. They simply *knew* more, and this unsettled the political establishment.

Even the fiery black preacher Theodore Vespers Love, known to friend and foe alike as T. V. Love, felt pressure to declare himself for or against specific policies that made sense for blacks. His speeches, traditionally demagogic and devoid of any program description, were beginning to draw increasing criticism from what had been his core constituency. The president, seeking a second term and heavily dependent upon black support, was deeply worried that blacks would abandon him because he'd lied on the card test taken before his first term. He tried to compensate by attending every conceivable event in the black community with blacks to whom he'd given jobs. It didn't work. The president lost his bid for a second term.

Honor was honor. Duty was duty. The card was the card.

Very little of this story actually happened. Maynard Jackson did, in fact, say to me, and I don't think facetiously, that a card of policy positions for blacks would be a good idea. But like so many good ideas, nothing came of it.*

The larger subtext of this allegorical story is its suggestion of a black community without a clear sense of direction, as if it were bogged in a muddy runnel, threading away from something memorable (the civil rights era) and toward something unseeable, with no sense of itself stout enough to see beyond the pale of another's interests, to find its own.

---

*It is important to note that more influential blacks than I can name here have committed their talents, money, and energies to worthwhile black community projects, more often than not to little public notice. Congressman Chaka Fattah has shepherded through a hostile Congress a bill to provide college scholarships for black students who would otherwise be unable to afford college. C. Dolores Tucker has fought to clean up rap lyrics. Gwendolyn Brooks has engaged a black publisher, Third World Press, for much of her work. Congresswoman Maxine Waters has worked to protect Caribbean economies from an insensitive Clinton administration. Ed Lewis, Earl Graves, Danny Glover, Bill and Camille Cosby, Ossie Davis, and Ruby Dee, among others, have given unstintingly of their time and money to a range of black social causes.

More generally still, our spirits are troubled by what we cannot remember and further by what we have little will to remember. Isn't it bitterly odd to reckon that blacks, of all people, can remember Moses but not his black Ethiopian wife, Zipporah? Or that *Beloved* failed commercially as a movie, in part, because blacks did not go to see it? I told my friend Walter Mosley, the writer, about blacks laughing during the movie's most wrenching scenes. He thought they had laughed because the blade reached too near to the bone, that the only part of our past that we have been allowed to know is a past too painful to visit. There are others who share Walter's view. I don't know. I have looked hard into my soul and I cannot see well enough around scarring caused by the same ugly forces that impelled them to laugh.

But I do know this. That even to muster the energy for a particularized broad new demand—to restore, to put back, to recompense—we will have to heal our spirits, for the most part, by ourselves.

6

RACE, MONEY, AND FOREIGN POLICY: THE CUBA EXAMPLE

I am now at risk of giving my life for my country's sake as is my duty, for it is thus that I understand it, and I am willing to timely prevent, with Cuba's independence, the United States from spreading across the Antilles and pouncing, with that added strength, on our America. Whatever I did to date, and will do in the future, is to that aim.

—José Martí, from an unfinished letter written the day before Martí was killed in the war against Spain for Cuban independence, May 18, 1895

PAIN BECAME NORMAL, flat, outstretching too long ago to know its origins and, thus, to contemplate its end. The social vistas of foreign travel have always helped me here with their conspicuous contrasts, their stimulating incongruities. I am caused to notice things at home I otherwise might not have. This has always been so with me. My January 1999 stay in Cuba only proved it again.

To many, the story may initially seem out of place because it is *foreign*. This is hardly the case. The United States is so unprecedentedly powerful that it can be best understood (even in its domestic race relations) when observed from without. Those who run America and benefit materially from its global hegemony regard the world as one place. So, then, must those around the globe who are subject to America's overwhelming social and economic influence. American racism is not merely a domestic social contaminant but a principal American export as well. The very notion of the nation-state has become little more than a convenient legal fiction or hiding place for anonymous and rapacious interests.

So, to Cuba.

It was after midnight when we left the Riviera Hotel, an art deco creation of American wise guys from the pre-Castro era. I had stayed there sixteen years before on my last visit to Cuba. Time and the American embargo had taken their toll. In 1989 the Soviet subsidy had ended, taking with it 35 percent of Cuba's gross national product. In 1992 U.S. Senator Robert Torricelli, a gnomish mean-spirit from New Jersey, had pushed through the United States Congress something called the Cuban Democracy Act which, among other things, banned international freighters from American ports for six months as punishment for stopping in Cuba to bring in or carry out trade goods. Not surprisingly, few freighters called at Havana. The once and future beautiful city creaked in merely surface disrepair.

We had been in Havana five days. Our chambermaid, whose name was María, had meticulously cleaned our large room, fruitlessly vacuuming the stained rug that had lain on the floor since inestimably before my last stay at the Riviera. The room was on the eighteenth floor and overlooked the ocean as it crashed into and over the Malecón, a four-lane avenue shielded by a three-foot-thick stone wall that protected the waterfront side of the city and seemed an apt metaphor for tiny Cuba's resolve to withstand indefinitely America's unrelenting economic hostility.

It was cool out, even for January. A young man and woman in sweaters walked hand in hand along the Malecón's sidewalk as ocean spray crested four stories above their heads before bathing the couple and a 1953 green and yellow four-door Chevrolet Bel Air sedan that was moving along in the lane nearest the ocean. The car listed to its right with a broken rear spring, as if it were dragging itself diagonally forward on its rump.

I had loved cars when I was a little boy in Richmond, Virginia. In the summer evenings I would sit endless hours on the wooden porch of my family's flat and count the cars moving along Third Street. I had known every make and model of everything that moved on wheels.

I knew the 1953 Chevy Bel Air backwards and forwards. It had been a simple and reliable car which sold new for less than twenty-five hundred dollars.

The car was forty-six years old. I didn't know when I'd last seen one. But there it was, puttering along the Malecón at midnight, a 1953 Bel Air, its dulled green and yellow paint spruced up by ocean spray raining from above.

As American cars go in Havana, the 1953 Bel Air was relatively modern. America's animus toward Cuba had followed closely on the heels of Castro's victory in 1959. Indeed the U.S. had begun to ratchet shut its trade doors *before* Cuba's new president had publicly declared Cuba a communist state. One could very nearly rough out the sequence of events for forty years past by watching the cars. Thousands, if not tens of thousands, of American cars crawling around Cuba. And not one made later than 1959. Humpback profiles from the 1940s. Swooping fenders from the 1950s. Cadillac's vintage fishtail editions. The much lamented Studebaker as helicopter facsimile. Packards, Nashes, Hudsons, Kaisers, De Sotos, Frazers— elsewhere all gone the way of the flightless dodo—running still in Cuba. Big whitewall tires with snakelike curb feelers, running boards, two-piece windshields. Ancient Plymouths with suicide doors that operated away from the center post like hard covers from a book's spine.

Cars are often the period marks of photojournalism. We use them to place ourselves in time. They help us with old undated photos. They provide era markers for filmmakers. This is why contemporary Cuba is so confusing to one's senses. The country's streets and roads are the closest thing extant to a time machine. Nostalgia live. The Hollywood set that isn't. No. Just a third-world island choked off by one nation, its powerful neighbor ninety miles to the north, the United States of America.

Forty years of unbroken economic assault, a Cuban cabinet minister had told us earlier in the day. The United States had decided to make an example of a nation of eleven million people. *Just say uncle.* But little Cuba had refused. And now its leader, only hours before the end of our visit, had invited us to his office for talks in the middle of the night.

We trudged onto our bus, a big ultramodern affair parked under the canopy of the hotel's circular driveway. The bus had been purchased in western Europe. I hadn't bothered to check the make and model but it could have come from anyplace except the U.S. The forty-year embargo had in the entire world one participant—us. But one participant was all that was needed when the *one* was the world's most powerful country and the country was next door.

Some of us had been sleeping (Hazel, Khalea, and me included) when the call came for the meeting. Danny Glover, the actor, and film producer Camille Cosby had been packing for flights scheduled to leave just after dawn, as had Harvard Medical School professors Alvin and Tina Poussaint. In fact, most in our delegation were booked on a 6:00 A.M. Mexicana Airways flight to Cancún. We had all been pressed into circuitous routes home because U.S. airlines do not fly to Cuba. The group that would get no sleep that night also included Walter Mosley, labor leaders William Lucy and William Fletcher, anthropologist Johnnetta Cole, and talk show host Tavis Smiley who had brought to Cuba with him a crew from Black Entertainment Television to document the events of our visit. Film director Carl Franklin would leave with my family and me on a flight later in the morning. Norman Francis, the president of Xavier University in New Orleans, and his wife, Blanche, planned to stay in Havana an extra day so that Blanche could spend more time with Cuban family members she had never met before our arrival five days thence.

In the 1930s Blanche's father had come from Cuba with his sister to attend Tuskegee Institute in Tuskegee, Alabama. After college he settled in the United States and started a family. His sister, Blanche's aunt, returned to Cuba. Blanche met her for the first time shortly after we arrived in Havana. She also met her octogenarian aunt's children and grandchildren.

I was touched watching them spend time like the most ordinary of close-knit families while reckoning with the gulf of lost years and an unfound lingua franca. While Blanche's story was special, we'd all felt something of an emotional connection to Cuba's blacks. We and they had borne much the same burden. Spanish slavery had lasted longer than our English variety and had been at least as cruel. Still, and somewhat paradoxically, race feels a lighter load in Cuba. The line that runs between colors is not so plainly visible as it is here. While here it cuts clean like a scissor, there it squirrels and fuzzes edgeless without stamina and vengeful purpose. I suspect that we may have the Moors to thank for this. They had stormed up from North Africa in the eighth century and subdued Spain and

Portugal before being repulsed in France. Although the Spanish and the Portuguese behaved during the slavery and colonial eras as abominably as the English, at least for them issues of blood prudery had long since been settled by the Moors. A *white* Cuban said to us, "I guess if you applied American definitions of race, we would all be Afro-Cubans." The statement surprised us. I must confess that it heartened me, although I was not sure why and was mildly embarrassed by the feeling.

In any case these were new feelings for us much abused African Americans. When the Afro-Cubans who had spent five days with us on the buses and in meetings insisted that race was not the same problem for them in Cuba that it was for us in America, we had some difficulty making ourselves believe it, although, as you can see, we very much wanted to. And support for their arguments seemed abundant enough and often in plain enough view. Thus we could do the requisite ancestor worship in Cuba that we, ourselves, could not do on the Mall in Washington.

General Antonio Maceo is a mythic figure in Cuba, rather comparable to America's founding fathers. A mammoth bronze likeness in downtown Havana invites recall of the revolutionary war heroism of a man who stands second only to José Martí in the pantheon of Cuban national heroes. Maceo was black. In Washington, I had never seen a major monument erected in memory of any black on any of the town's prized quadrangles. But here in Cuba rising above a major square stood a majestic Maceo. I stared at it for a good long time, I guess as much for its novelty (to me at least) as its message. Maceo, wounded in battle against the Spaniards on more than twenty occasions, was said to have had steely courage and an iron will. The bronze mustachioed face jutted in a dare and seemed to prove the reputation.

Such thoughts swam through my head as I took a seat with Hazel in the back of the darkened bus. The visit to Cuba had caused me to think a great deal about America and the static character of its various racial separations. I had seen it from Havana more clearly because Havana was such a dramatic cultural departure from America.

This is not to idealize the Cubans on race matters. White Cubans still appear very much to have the better of things. They dominate political power. They are generally better off economically. But having acknowledged such legacies of Cuban inequality, anyone with half a brain must conclude that their chances of an equal society are infinitely better than ours. For whatever reason (a bequest of the Moors or not) Cubans seem qualitatively less racist than Americans. *White* Cubans, as I have said, talk with unremarkable emphasis about their African ancestry. I think Hazel would rather I not write this because I appear to imply that I am pleased by such talk. I think many of us *were*, and that in itself, I confess, is puzzling.

It could be, as well, that a lot of what one hears on these matters from Cuban government officials has more to do with the head than the heart—ideology as opposed to sincere open-mindedness, so to speak. I cannot know the answer to this. I do know that white Americans don't talk or think like this, and the end of manifest racism in America can only begin with such talk and thought. At the same time, it is not lost on me that no such avowals were widely heard around white Cuba *before* 1959 or in white Cuban Miami even now. But, whatever their motivation, white Cubans in Cuba sound sincere on matters of race.

I have never been inclined to make predictions, but it requires little courage to forecast that the embargo will be lifted within three years. There is a growing chorus of disparate voices calling for it. I can't recall ever agreeing with Henry Kissinger about anything, but even he has called for a review of American policy. This is probably driven in his case by despair over lost American business opportunities. His overture, joined in by two other former secretaries of state, was spurned however by the Clinton administration. The objections, I was told, came from Vice President Al Gore. The story goes that he was fearful of losing the political support of anti-Castro Cubans concentrated in southern Florida, from whom he received money for his bid for the presidency. Still, the policy tides are now discernible and, I think, inexorable. Relations between the United States and Cuba will lurch toward normalization, the vice president's political flaccidity notwithstanding. And with normalization, Americans will flock to Havana. It is a stunning city that one feels, behind the embargo curtain, oddly privileged to see. The architecture, suggestive of sixteenth-century Spain and touched by Greek Revival themes, is marred only (as virtually all cities lamentably are) by the boxy structures conceived and stuccoed in this century. The principal arteries are four-lane affairs bisected by broad grassy esplanades under canopies of brilliant flamboyant trees and towering royal palms. Mansions that were once the homes of the wealthy who decamped for Florida in 1959 now house behind bougainvillea-clad walls public service organizations and restaurants tastefully devoid of neon signage.

After five days our delegation had gelled into something of a family. We had been steadfastly serious in our meetings and often somewhat zany in our on-the-bus comportment. (I confess that I was as much a leader in the latter as the former. Humor is nature's preservative of the spirit and I'd have gone batty long ago without it.)

We had five miles or so to travel to government headquarters. The night and the bus were quiet. A lone car, a 1956 Cadillac, moved alongside. Its fishtail lights had ceased to function and the car's owner had affixed two free-standing lights to the rear fender deck above the dead originals.

With us on the bus were four Afro-Cubans, one of whom, Felix Wilson Hernández, I'd known well enough and long enough during his tenure at the Cuban Interest Section in Washington to call a friend. The United States has, unlike the rest of the world, only vestigial diplomatic relations with Cuba. This diplomacy, if one could call it that, is conducted by the Cubans from a building on Sixteenth Street staffed by fewer than fifteen people, including Felix, first secretary and deputy chief of the section. By contrast the U.S. Interest Section in Havana is larger (with a staff of forty-seven) than any American embassy facility in the Caribbean archipelago of thirteen countries. Considering that our officials in Havana are not spending their time on trade facilitation chores, one doesn't have to work very hard to imagine just what it is that is claiming their time. Normally, influential Americans visiting Havana are contacted by the Interest Section before or shortly after their arrival. To my knowledge, no one in our delegation had been contacted. At least Hazel and I had not. I guessed that we had been written off as lost causes.

Felix was seated on the aisle five rows forward of our seats talking quietly to Carl Franklin, the film director. Carl was one of only two members of our delegation, Bill Fletcher of the AFL-CIO being the other, whom I had not known before the trip. They had been recommended to me by Walter Mosley and Bill Lucy respectively, and both had added much to the quality of our discussions.

Johnnetta Cole sat on an aisle near the front next to her husband, Arthur Robinson, an official with the National Institutes of Health, and across from Orlaida Cabrera Gutiérrez. While I had been to Cuba three times before, for Johnnetta it seemed a virtual homecoming. She had known for years many of the people who had received us at the airport, including Orlaida. My recall is that Johnnetta had a better Spanish proficiency than any of us, with Hazel placing a distant second. Johnnetta had not only visited Cuba often, she had actually lived there during the 1970s while working for a period in the Venceremos Brigade. I think she had known Orlaida from as long ago as that.

Like the other Afro-Cubans aboard, Orlaida worked for the American section of Cuba's foreign ministry. She was of compact physical stature, with a warm, engaging manner uncompromised by her obvious leadership suits. She in fact had full responsibility for implementing our schedule of meetings and site visits. (Here I feel the urge to say something about the chemistry between us and our immediate Afro-Cuban hosts, but first let me finish rounding out the picture of them, albeit sketchily.)

The first thing that one notices about Adelina Allen Hilton is the striking dark beauty of a type seen often in Senegal, where complexions have a uniquely textured black depth and richness to them. Adelina, tall and runway-slender, seemed completely unaware of such corporeal qualities and comported herself with a shy quietness that revealed over the short term little about her. By contrast, Marcelino Fajardo was tall and gray-haired with a voice presence ample for the Shakespearean stage. While I can't be certain what all of their official roles were, Adelina appeared to be subordinate to Orlaida, while Marcelino played a role at least collateral to hers. As for Felix, known well on both sides, I had requested before leaving Washington that he be present in Havana during our visit.

You may sense from the tone of this that we had grown, by day five of our trip, close to our black hosts—that we had allowed them into positions of some social trust that even white Americans likely would not have been allowed to enter, at least so uncircumspectly. Though this assessment was entirely unvoiced, it was entirely the case nonetheless. Afro-Cubans we'd never seen before, whose language most of us could not speak, whose political creeds our American political leaders had unreservedly condemned, had become something close to friends.

Gullible, some would say. Well, I think not. The head tells. The head hears. The head believes or disbelieves. But the viscera *know*. Especially viscera trained in pain as, sadly, ours had been for as far back in time any of us could remember. Think what you will, but this was our reaction—which, in any case, says more about race relations in America than about anything about Cuba. And that is, in essence, why I have chosen to write about our time in Cuba before my memory of it dims.

To be sure, I had my doubts—I suppose all of us did—about the truth of much of what we had heard, even from the Afro-Cubans with us on the bus that night. While some Afro-Cubans with whom we met had denied the existence of racism in Cuba, most had not. Even Castro himself would speak of it to us later as a persistent and stubborn social problem warranting an equally persistent government response beyond the mere application of law.

The larger point, however, was this. We would not stay in Cuba long enough to sort fact from fiction, good from bad, in the Cuban government's picture of itself and its programs, not even after listening to Felix, Orlaida, Adelina, and Marcelino. We could not know in such a short time what Cuba *was*. But we *could* know that it was not what American officials had said it was, or perhaps, more important, had *not* said it was. We could also know from direct witness what the United States was doing to these people, most of whom were black and innocent of anything, least of all harm to the United States.

We were sure that Cuba had some human rights problems, but where were they on a scale of one to ten? We ourselves had been victims of American human rights violations. From that perspective, Cuba felt better.

Of course, it might have been that we knew America too well and Cuba not well enough. I will concede this, and further concede that, insofar as the overall picture of the place is concerned, I can only report with any surety how the feel of Cuba settled on our senses. And even there, in an effort to be what no one can be in our particular fix, namely *objective*, I will say what few of us will say aloud, even when we have crystallized the emotion in a conscious phrase:

Many blacks—most, perhaps, though I can't be sure—don't like America.

Oh, we often like its wealth, its abundance of commodities, its markets of endless stuff, its constitutional freedoms, but we are angrier than many would think, having been treated so badly for so long. We are, indeed, at least full citizens with rights and we are not going anywhere else. But we are emotional defectors from a society whose white majority long ago smothered to death any notion of cultural co-ownership. And then papered the deed with lies. Lies of commission. Lies of omission. Lies to the world and to ourselves about the world and ourselves, told through the vast electronic machines of interrelated private interests by those who serve *theirs* and ignore anyone else's. Lies about our various national social pathologies: urban, class, and racial. Distorted in the telling. Buried in the untelling.

I have seen oppressive societies and felt them firsthand with the trustable senses. In Libya, no one I encountered was willing to talk about Muammar Qaddafi. Libyans seemed frightened by the mere mention of the man whose ubiquitous picture appeared in my Tripoli hotel lobby in at least five places. South Africa's apartheid society reeked with the menace of its ugly racialism. Even on the eve of Zimbabwe's independence in 1980, white security agents lurking among the crush of dignitaries staying at the Monomatapa Hotel craned their necks to overhear and report to the British colony's outgoing white-rule masters the piecemeal utterances of the country's soon-to-be black leaders.

Cuba felt like none of this. But while in five days I had seen fewer than ten men bearing arms anywhere in Havana city and province, I am reluctant to render a conclusive measurement in fear that my judgment may not be broadly enough informed by long on-site experience. I choose to stick to what I saw and what I know. It is all I can do, given the welter of American half-truths and untruths that have entangled the story of Cuba for at least a century.

Even as long ago as 1898 during Cuba's war of independence against Spain, American politicians apparently bent the truth in service to their own narrow ambitions. As a child, I had heard accounts and seen pen-and-ink illustrations of Teddy

Roosevelt leading his Rough Riders up San Juan Hill in a glorious cavalry charge that would do much to burnish the growing myth of Roosevelt as a fearless (and electable) adventurer. The writer Elmore Leonard describes a somewhat less heroic tableau in the novel *Cuba Libre* through the character of Neely Tucker, a *Chicago Times* war correspondent who says:

"... there was no mounted cavalry during the campaign; all the horses had been left at Port Tampa, though some staff and division officers had horses. Teddy, as a matter of fact, brought along two, one called Little Texas and another, Rain-in-the-Face, named for an Indian Chief. Teddy did take Kettle Hill, but by the time he got to the San Juan Heights the battle was almost over. . . . I saw it as ironic that regular-army Negro soldiers, members of the 9th and 10th Colored Cavalry, were made to unload the Rough Riders' gear from the ship while Teddy and his volunteers, amateurs, really, march off to meet the enemy. And when they walked into an ambush, at Las Guasimas, it was the colored boys along with the 71st Infantry who came along to prevent Teddy's boys from being wiped out."

Indeed, the February 15, 1898, sinking of the U.S. battleship *Maine* in Havana harbor, the incident that brought the U.S. quickly into what had been a war between Spain and its colony, Cuba, is still one of history's most intriguing whodunits. Many at the time conjectured that the United States, the power with the most to gain from the *Maine*'s demise, had sabotaged its own ship as a pretext for protecting American investments and staking a hegemonic claim on Cuba. According to Elmore Leonard, most of the ship's crew were blacks. All of its officers were white and all had gone ashore before the explosions occurred that took the ship to the harbor's bottom. This, of course, did nothing to diminish suspicion. The boat sinking would hand to the U.S. a nice little war with overmatched Spain that would be over in three months' time and yield up to Washington, as spoils, protectorate authority over Cuba and jurisdiction over Puerto Rico and the Philippines as well.

American public discourse being inherently dishonest (as, likely, is everyone else's), I try to confine myself to judgments that can be proved from observation and primary research.

———

The child sat on a thinly padded gurney pushed against a gray wall of the poorly lit treatment room. She was four years old, small for her age, and gaunt. Her skin was sallow, her eyes big in the small face, a visage of ineffable sadness.

I don't recall that the middle-aged Afro-Cuban physician gave the child's name as he described her condition to us. He had spoken in English and the child had given no indication that she understood any of what was being said either by the physician or by the black Americans standing in a small crowd before her.

"She was born with a hole in one of her interior heart walls. Her pumped blood moves in the wrong direction, creating pressure in the lungs. She suffers, as a result, from pulmonary hypertension. We can repair the hole in the heart wall, but her lungs will need to be replaced or she will die."

The child sat in unnatural stillness as if husbanding her strength.

"Do you do organ transplants in Cuba?" asked Dr. Alvin Pouissaint of Harvard Medical School.

"We can do them for adults, but we are not yet able to do them for children."

Given the circumstances of U.S.-Cuban relations, we interpreted this answer as a death sentence.

Virtually nothing passes between the small island nation and its powerful neighbor ninety miles to the North. The American government has so thoroughly demonized the Castro regime that Americans see no downside to this. But the consequences of Washington's animus would be apparent enough to even a casual visitor to Havana's William Soler Pediatric Cardiology Hospital. Antiquated diagnostic equipment. Shortages of antibiotics, plasma, surgical instruments, and catheters. Surgical gloves, intended for a single use, washed and reused, rewashed and used again.

The dying girl on the gurney would not likely penetrate America's blockade to receive the operation that could save her life.

Hers is not an isolated case. Child cancer patients in Cuba routinely endure excruciating distress because American sanctions deny Cuban health care providers access to nearly half of the new world-class drugs available in a global pharmaceutical market dominated by American producers. In an earlier visit to a similar pediatric ward, officials of the American Association for World Health found that thirty-five children undergoing chemotherapy had been vomiting twenty-eight to thirty times a day because the U.S. embargo had prevented access to metoclopramide, a nausea-preventing drug. In another ward, a five-year-old girl without Implantofix bore nearly unendurable pain because her veins had collapsed and her chemotherapy had to be administered through her jugular vein.

In the meeting toward which we were driving through the

night, I would ask President Fidel Castro about the small reforms President Clinton had made in the sanctions policy.

"As soon as President Clinton announced his change in policy regarding medicine," he answered, "we sent to Washington a list of medicines that we wanted to buy. We have not received so much as a single aspirin."

And yet, drawing on wellsprings of fierce determination, Cuba has somehow survived America's onslaught with its programs for universal health care and education intact, an infant mortality rate as low as America's (half that of Washington, D.C.), a life expectancy as long as America's, and a literacy rate that is the highest in Latin America. In the teeth of Washington's still-escalating official hatred—deepened in recent years by further punitive measures pushed forward by Congressman Dan Burton, Senator Jesse Helms, and Senator Torricelli—Cuba has persevered. "We have not closed one school," said Castro, his soft voice containing a depth of emotion his vigorous gesticulations appeared to evidence.

TransAfrica Forum's delegation to Cuba had drawn from a broad variety of disciplines: education, medicine, organized labor, human rights advocacy, journalism, and the arts. We had come to gauge the ground-level human cost of our country's sanctions to the Cuban people, and particularly to the Afro-Cubans who comprise more than half of Cuba's population. After all, like us, they had suffered through centuries of slavery followed by racial segregation. This had ended for them only in 1959 with the overthrow of General Fulgencio Batista's regime by Fidel Castro.

Because education and health care in Cuba are universally accessible and free, blacks who had been victims of slavery and ensuing racial discrimination have benefited disproportionately from Castro's social policies, as have the country's poor generally. On the other hand, not surprisingly, these most vulnerable sectors of Cuban society have also borne the brunt of America's hostility.

Among the American products embargoed for export to Cuba is food. What the United States refuses to sell is greatly more expensive and difficult to obtain elsewhere. The problem was exacerbated for Cuba by the collapse of the Soviet Union in 1991, resulting in the loss of Havana's export earnings from Moscow and the shrinkage of Cuba's economy by a third. Between 1989 and 1993 the daily intake of calories in Cuba also fell by a third, and not fortuitously.

Although suffering and needless deaths have been widespread, Cuba's structurally excellent health care delivery system has spared the country a humanitarian catastrophe as the government has increased health spending by shifting funds from other departments like defense, culture, the arts, and administration.

But why the enduring embargo that seemed to all of us in Havana nothing short of cruel? Why is our country—alone in the world, against the call of Pope John Paul II and the entire family of nations—crucifying this small, largely black country of eleven million people?

While I have no certain answer of my own, I do know the answer is not what has been told to the American people by U.S. presidents from Eisenhower to Clinton.

Clearly, the reason is not simply that Cuba is a communist country. China is a communist country and the United States not only declines to punish China for its communism or for its deplorable human rights record but grants it most-favored-nation status besides. Indeed, in April 1996 China appears to have stolen from the United States secrets for making warheads small enough for clustering on long-range missiles. Although this was reported to President Clinton's national security advisor fairly promptly, the suspected spy, Wen Ho Lee, a Chinese American scientist at the Los Alamos nuclear research laboratory, was not fired until March 1999 after failing an FBI polygraph test and refusing to cooperate with a bureau investigation of how the Chinese had gained information ten years before about the Navy's newest strategic warhead, the W-88. And even when the story finally did break, it was the Clinton administration that was smoothing ruffled Chinese feathers, not the other way around.

So communism, aggressive or benign, couldn't have been Cuba's unforgivable sin. Indeed, the Eisenhower administration had become hostile to the Castro government even before it had reason to believe Castro *was* a communist. As Tad Szulc writes in *Fidel* (1986):

> Even before Eisenhower policy-makers began to understand what was happening in Cuba ... a top-level decision was made to get rid of Castro. Specifically [in] the secret agenda of the National Security Council meeting on March 10, 1959— two and a half months after Batista's defeat ... The Cubans had not yet seized or nationalized any American property on the island, and the United States had no reason thus far to complain about any Cuban actions. ... It remains a mystery why the National Security Council discussed Castro's liquidation within five days of his first encounter with the American Ambassador without giving diplomacy a chance.

If the United States hadn't isolated Cuba because of its communism, it just as certainly hadn't done it because of Cuba's human rights record. While Cuba has a one-party system and suppresses dissent (not surprising, given our forty-year American effort to overthrow their government and kill Castro), Cuba has a better record with respect to human rights than many of the Latin American governments that the United States has steadfastly supported, let alone Batista's regime whose police and soldiers killed and tortured thousands of its opponents.

In 1954, Secretary of State John Foster Dulles arranged with his brother, Allen Dulles, CIA director, and the United Fruit Company (now Chiquita Brands) to overthrow the democratically elected government of Guatemala. In the years afterwards, a Guatemalan truth commission now reveals, the United States provided financial aid and training to Guatemalan army units that killed more than 200,000 civilians from 1960 to 1996.

On March 7, 1999, the *New York Times* reported:

> Newly declassified American documents, for example, place a C.I.A. officer in the room where Guatemalan intelligence officers—men responsible for death squad killings—planned their covert operations in 1965. They show that C.I.A. and other American officials played a key role in the latter 1960's in centralizing command structures and communications of agencies that would be involved in death squad killings for years. . . .
>
> They also show that the C.I.A. station in Guatemala City knew that the Guatemalan army was massacring entire Mayan villages while Reagan administration officials publicly supported the military regime's human rights record. Even after the war was won, the documents reveal, Defense Intelligence

Agency officials knew that the Guatemalan military was destroying evidence of torture centers and clandestine graveyards in 1994. Not a word was uttered publicly by the Clinton Administration.

(Possibly the *Times* tipped the balance. Three days later, while on a visit to Guatemala, President Clinton apologized directly to Guatemalan officials for United States support for right-wing governments over the years in that country.)

During Argentina's military dictatorships of the 1970s and 1980s, more than 15,000 Argentines "disappeared." The U.S. never flinched. In Chile, General Augusto Pinochet killed at least three thousand civilians in the aftermath of overthrowing a democratic government. The CIA helped him come to power. The FBI helped him stay there.

So it's not about human rights either.

Why then does the United States, alone in the world, hate Cuba so? I suspect the answer has, more than anything else, to do with property and cheek. The former, Castro seized from the rich and put at the disposal of the poor. The latter, Castro already had in abundance. In the eyes of an arrogant American officialdom, both are unpardonable sins.

The world has increasingly come to see the U.S. embargo against Cuba as a violation of the United Nations Charter. And our delegation, if of a common opinion on little else, was unanimous in the view that the embargo was inhumane and should be lifted forthwith. For what human right could be more basic than the right of access to food and medicine? To deny such essentials to people who bore Americans no malice was to cover us all in shame.

But few Americans knew enough about Cuba to quarrel with

America's policies. Indeed, in the public's hierarchy of satans, Castro had been placed right alongside Saddam Hussein. Yet I, who had traveled throughout the world and seen unfeeling tyrants close-up, had never seen one who focused meager public resources on programs for universal health care and education. Who has? Have you? Policymakers here never denied that Castro's government had done such things. They didn't have to, because no one in our general public knew it anyhow. Virtual information as a product of an untold but irrefutable truth. Living behind a wall, are we, smug in our knowledge of nothing, pummeling the small enemy at the behest of the self-interested well-placed few whose interests are most assuredly not ours. How do you get to know anything, when everything you are allowed to know is distilled, shaped, edited, and ultimately permitted by news industries in private hands—hands naturally sympathetic to those Castro had unburdened in 1959? I am not making a case here for state owned news industries. That has been proved to result in even more disastrous consequences. I want simply to have the American public discover what it likely doesn't know is there—its cavernous blind spot, lost in which are the festering angers of the world's invisible. And their first appeal is for simple acknowledgment. *We are here. We are in pain. Our problems have causes. The causes can be known.*

With an acid humor, I likened the privacy of such unlit suffering to a sign printed in English above the door of the American commercial aircraft on which I had flown part of the way to Cuba: "If not able to speak or understand English, please notify the crew."

What?

As I traveled in Cuba, my soul remembered that somewhere, long ago, Sir Walter Scott had written the lines

Breathes there the man, with soul so dead,
Who never to himself hath said,
This is my own, my native land!

African Americans had never been allowed to own the *idea* of America. Had never been allowed to glimpse in its mirror the complex whole of the ancient self they had presented to it. Had never known a moment's grant of respite at home from the mean burden of race. Had danced in shadows to tunes strummed never for them.

And thus we knew, unremarked, a pre-existing friendship with our Afro-Cuban hosts. For they, like us, had been America's victims, and beneath the false policy babble, for many of the same reasons.

***

The bus growled through the night. No one talked. A few caught catnaps. The overhead reading lights were all off. That and the quiet of the big city's streets gave a peace in which to ruminate.

It is odd seeing Lenin's portrait in public places. People calling themselves communists as if it were really, really all right to say such a thing aloud. I wonder if they really are communists. I mean Felix and Orlaida and the others. Strange the grip of socialization. I don't think I could ever have been a communist, so well have the acquisitive appetites been nourished in my family of wants. But one doesn't have to be a communist, I guess, to see Americans as overly materialistic. The time Hazel and I tried to buy a poinciana tree in St. Kitts from a very old man sitting on his front porch with his very old wife. He looked poor. The house was modest. But you can never tell about these things. Multimillionaires live in modest structures. This seems strange to me still. The poinciana tree was in a field far from his little house. I remember thinking we could quickly agree on a price for the tree standing on untamed land. Turned out, the old man owned large tracts of land, had robust holdings, and he very nicely, but firmly, told us that he was not at all interested in selling the poinciana tree at any price. We tested an outrageous offer we'd never have paid and found the old man on his little porch to mean exactly what he had said. I guess there are many noncommunist societies where money is not everything or even mostly everything.

Those early Christians, now they were communists. Saint Paul and a band of believers traveled after Jesus' crucifixion throughout Asia Minor and Syria spreading the word that eternal salvation was available to any who believed in Jesus. Their writings reveal that they opposed all notions of private property-holding. The lending of money with interest was seen as a breach of the faith. Unholy. Usurious. They were communalists. What little they had, belonged to them equally. They were commune-ists or communists as the word later evolved. The global superpower of the time, the Romans, considered such teachings subversive, banned them, and prosecuted those who continued to observe their young faith in secret. Many of the stubborn Christians were thrown into arenas with wild beasts to be killed. By 393 A.D., Christianity, its tenets apparently long since tempered by the Roman sanctions, had become the official religion of the Roman Empire.

————

The bus approached the handsome gates of the government compound. We started forward on a generally uphill trajectory

————

along a driveway that undulated through a sloping expanse of manicured lawn dotted by stately royal palms. This was my second visit to the compound. Like the visit sixteen years ago, our meeting would begin in the middle of the night. The untraditional scheduling has never been explained to me and I can make no informed guess about the reasons for it. I mention it only because darkness on both of my visits circumscribed my ability to judge the size of the fenced compound or how many structures it accommodated. As it was, the only building I could see was an attractive and large low-rise modern edifice sheathed in what appeared under the landscape and accent lights to be white marble. I realized after the bus pulled to a stop before the sheltered entrance that this was the building in which the president's office was located, where I had met with him before.

We surrendered hand and camera bags to security officials in the carpeted foyer before being taken to a large rectangular reception room with high ceilings and tasteful appointments. No more than five minutes had elapsed before our bags were returned to us. The room was large enough to accept six or more furniture groupings of sofas, armchairs, and coffee tables arranged around the perimeter, leaving open at the room's center an area that must have measured thirty by forty feet.

Moments after our bags had been returned to us, the eight-foot double doors near the end of the room's long side opened and in strode President Castro followed by an attractive woman who had been his translator on the occasion of our last meeting. The members of our group stood as Hazel, Khalea, and I walked across the room to greet the Latin American leader who had for forty years tweaked the nose of the most powerful nation on earth and gotten away with it. Whatever else he had accomplished, this Jesuit-trained revolutionary had exempted his country of eleven million from all of Washington's banana-republic jokes. For American officials Fidel Castro was no laughing matter.

More than four decades before, he had launched with seven guns an armed revolt against Batista's U.S.-armed eighty-thousand-man force. He had survived the shipwreck of the badly overloaded thirty-eight-foot *Granma*, en route from a self-exile of military training in Mexico with a tiny invasion force of eighty-two expeditionaries, only to be trapped by Batista's soldiers in a cane field for five days and five nights, hiding under layers of sugarcane leaves without food or water, enduring by sucking sugar syrup from the stalks while supine and covered, whispering to his men in the night, "We are winning . . . victory will be ours." He had earlier risked the entire expedition while searching the tall night sea for hours in an effort to rescue Roberto Roque, who had slipped and fallen overboard. In bad weather, using only a lantern, they had incredibly, found Roque alive. Castro thereupon proclaimed to his very seasick men that they were now on their way to victory. Scarcely two years later, he would ride with his men into Havana, victorious, with the unquestioned support of Cuba's peasants.

Clearly, this was no ordinary man.

He was a year younger than I am now, when I had last seen him. He was seventy-two now. Time is the foe to which even the most indomitable of wills must submit. The bearing was the same, however, as were the eyes that all but told you how the near impossible had been accomplished in the Sierra Maestra so long ago.

Tall and wearing dress fatigues, Castro moved around the

room, meeting all of his guests before leading the way down a long corridor to a meeting room.

We arranged ourselves around a hardwood conference table with the members of our delegation taking up a long side and both ends. President Castro sat at the center of the opposite long side and directly across from me. To his right was Ricardo Alarcón de Quesada, the president of the National Assembly, who appeared to be in his mid-sixties. Alarcón, along with two other Cuban officials and three or four of our number, wore a business suit and necktie. Of the Cubans, only the president wore military clothes. The rest of the men, including me, were informally dressed in sports jackets and open collars. To Castro's left was the translator, whose intonation and pace mirrored the president's.

In the beginning, his voice was very soft. Even wistful. It may have been nothing more than a technique of his, but I didn't think so at the time. He seemed tired. He started to talk about the past as if he were talking to himself. The index finger of his left hand stabbed the air in counterpoint to the mildness of his voice.

"We began the struggle with seven guns against eighty thousand soldiers under arms. . . . We had learned to take the weapons from the enemy. . . . After the revolution, all of our credits were cancelled. Our accounts in the United States were blocked. The blockade began before 1959."

He paused, no longer seeming tired. His eyes shone with intelligent intensity.

"But there is no insurmountable obstacle. . . . [The embargo] has turned us into patriots, into men and women. I think we are better now. . . . [Before the revolution] thirty percent were illiterate. Sixty percent were semiliterate. Just five percent with schooling. Only 50,000 Cubans had more than a fifth-grade education. Now there are 250,000 teachers, 600,000 university graduates, 54,000 doctors."

He believed, as he had reason to, that he could will a result. The young man in the cane field—*we are winning . . . victory will be ours*. And his will seemed still a veritable force-field. Though he was not a young seventy-two, the failing body gave glimpse through the eyes to an inferno of intellect and determination. He had lost nothing there.

I reflected that, with such sustained powers of purpose and reckoning, he had to have been beset from time to time by bouts of despondency. The young revolutionary had planned to move his country away from a dependence on sugar, to diversify the economy. He had failed. He could not *will* away the American embargo which guaranteed this particular failure. He had banished prostitution and pretty much done away with urban street crime. But even such conditions as these came to be beyond any one man's will to control in this *special period*. (The Cubans have a wonderful talent for understating difficulty.) A third of their economy, overnight, gone with the Soviet wind, and Castro saying, still softly but now defiantly, "When the gates were closed and the Soviet Union collapsed, it was inconceivable that we would last a week. . . . We have lasted now about three thousand days waiting for the news."

But there had been painful costs, like those I have already described to you. And the prostitutes outside our hotel had not been there sixteen years before. He had been saying to us without emphasis, "With the opening of the country, we have had an increase in crime." The dollar now filling the fissures opened by America's crushing embrace, verticalizing anew a society the man before us had spent his life trying to equalize.

I wondered if he felt just a little trapped, with only the short string of his time left to play out, force-fed the bitter fruit of blame for his people's current suffering. Suffering for which the U.S., not he, should have had to bear the major responsibility. Life is seldom kind or fair to social dreamers.

He went on in quiet reminiscence about the social goals he had labored four decades to achieve—all now coming unstuck through circumstances beyond his control, and with no fair court of American public opinion in which to plead his case. I listened with a conflicted reflex. He had been demonized so in my American diet of ideas and information. The Cubans who had left Cuba upon his arrival hated him. But there had been no bloodbath, as for instance with Suharto in Indonesia. Suharto's army had slaughtered a reported half million people. But Suharto was never demonized as Castro had been, and Castro's victorious army had acquitted itself by all accounts with discipline and forbearance.

I told myself more than once as I listened to him that very likely in the world only Americans evaluated Castro in this most severely blinkered way. On the occasion of former Jamaican prime minister Michael Manley's funeral in Kingston in March of 1998, something akin to a murmur ran through the crowd of thousands upon Castro's approach to the Anglican Kingston Parish Church: *Fidel is coming. Fidel is coming.* As it turned out, he was the only foreign dignitary to receive a standing ovation from a crowd that had assembled in the church to celebrate the life of a Jamaican who had devoted his gifts to quests for global social justice.

And still a few ordinary Cuban Americans I had talked to seemed to hate Castro. I was troubled by this, finding their passion as inexplicable as that of white American truck drivers who had supported Ronald Reagan. The Cuban Americans claimed that Castro had rendered Cuba an "unfree" country. But had they thought Cuba a freer society before Castro? When America liked it? When Cuba was racially segregated? When education was only available to a privileged few? When the poor died of easily curable ailments? When vice was rampant? Had they preferred Batista's mafia-infested Cuba? Or the Cuba between the state that Teddy Roosevelt preened to subjugate and Franklin Delano Roosevelt worked to keep?

There was hardly a thoughtful observer in the hemisphere who did not believe that Cuba all but belonged to the United States. As Sir Eric Williams wrote in *From Columbus to Castro*:

The situation was more discouraging in Cuba, which was in every sense of the term an American colony. The Americans openly supported, in the interest of stability, the dictator Machado who raised no awkward questions of Cuban independence and who was concerned merely with the exile or assassination of hostile labour leaders and the reckless and enormous increase of the public debt, both public and private. America dominated the scene. One American writer has stated that no one could become President of Cuba without the endorsement of the United States. According to another, the American Ambassador in Havana was the most important man in Cuba. A third analyses United States policy as "putting a veto on revolution whatever the cause". The Platt Amendment dominated the relations between the United States and Cuba. On the occasion of a threatened rebellion by a Negro political party, the Independent Party of Colour, the United States sent troops to Cuba. In reply to Cuba's protests Secretary of State Knox stated: "The United States does not undertake first to consult the Cuban Government if a crisis arises requiring a temporary landing somewhere." In 1933 Ambassador Sumner Welles identified six desirable characteristics which a Cuban president should possess. These read in part: "First, his thorough acquaintance with the desires of this Government. . . . Sixth, his amenability to suggestions or advice which might be made to him by the American Legation."

Such had been the terms of American policy toward Cuba for more than sixty years beyond the close of Spanish colonialism. Until Castro.

Washington had heartily supported a parade of corrupt, cruel, and dictatorial Cuban governments up until 1959. It had virtually run them. It had ignored their protean venalities, their slimy underbellies, and sidled up in ugly collaboration. American tourists had slept in swank new hotels, gambled in garish palaces, frolicked at the Tropicana, never noticing the Cuba that was racially segregated and deeply class-skewed. Seeing buildings. Never really the people, the extras. Never the misery.

Then *he* arrived. And with (whatever it may have been originally) an idea of his own.

This had maddened Americans. Made them crazy, like some consciousness-altering brew rendering circles square and squares oblong. Look at a thing dead on, and flat not see it. See a thing, quite literally, that wasn't there. If our government decided to hate *him* for declining to play the Latin cipher, our people with small inspiration decided to hate him for stuff they would just make up, without, I think, knowing they were fabricating rationales for their reflexive antipathies. Their comments would quite frequently make them look silly, but not to each other because they believed what they were saying no matter how baseless. Nice people, even, said these things. Not lying, because I believe they thought they were telling the truth.

Of course the stories, owing to repetition, had become a kind of truth and proliferated less examined than before.

We were witness to samples of such malignant blather when the Baltimore Orioles played in Havana against the Cuban national team on March 28, 1999. Baseball Hall of Famer and ESPN analyst Joe Morgan, with stunning illogic, said to an American viewing audience: "[Cubans] don't have access to information [about American baseball] but they get it." Indeed, Cubans know a great deal more about American baseball than Americans know about baseball in Cuba, which is next to nothing.

Thomas Boswell, sports columnist for the *Washington Post*, wrote of Havana: "Of course, almost every structure you can see from your panoramic picture window looks like it's been neutron-bombed." What quality of anger drives such extreme and, in this case, wholly unwarranted hyperbole? Havana is an attractive city in need of cosmetic repairs in a developing country saddled with shortages occasioned by our country's economic embargo. Faced with the choice of investing scarce resources in people or paint, the government chose people.

Boswell went on to write: "Maybe it's because there are no clocks in Cuba. In two days, not one clock has come into view anywhere."

Of course this is absurd and I feel somewhat diminished to need report to you that on my several visits to Cuba, the country was awash with clocks. Digital clocks in every hotel room I'd ever stayed in. Moon-faced clocks in public places. Clocks on wrists. And I hardly think Cuban officials would go to the trouble of concentrating all the country's timepieces on the walls and night tables and wrists I might likely have seen. But perhaps they might have, had they known that among all the many charges leveled at them by Americans, clocklessness would one day find its way into print.

A *Washington Post* staff writer, Richard Justice, wrote that "team executives jammed into a ramshackle airport this morning to board a charter flight back to the United States." There are grounds on which the Cuban government deserves criticism. But why the petty whole-cloth invention? Havana's airport is a spanking brand-new state-of-the-art facility.

Alisa Valdes-Rodriguez, a *Los Angeles Times* writer, wrote: "Havana smells like a jar of vaseline and if you stand outside for more than fifteen minutes, your skin gets coated with black goo." This is but a snippet of a screed that appeared in the *Washington Post*. Why would so widely respected a newspaper as the *Washington Post* print writing so palpably counterfactual as this? Havana does not smell like anything or anyplace in particular. In fact, I don't recall that it even has a smell. And one doesn't have to be a pulmonary disease specialist to see that Havanans would not survive to an average age of five, not to speak of seventy-two, were they inhaling black goo. But the *tar mist* or *black goo vapor* description of Cuba is likely a first-use description of any country's urban environment. Havana's air is as clean as any major city's air (and markedly cleaner than the smog-laden air Ms. Valdes-Rodriguez breathes in Los Angeles).

In this vein, I've always marveled at the consistency with which American mainstream journalists write about African cities as "dusty." Not South African cities, mind you, but all the rest south of the Sahara. "Ghana's dusty capital of Accra" or "the dusty seaside city of Dar es Salaam." It goes on and on. In any long print-news piece, Africa's cities will invariably be described to Americans as "dusty." To drive the point home (when digressing, in for the penny, in for the pound), how would Americans feel if every foreign news reference to an American city in publications like Paris's *Le Monde*, Kingston's *Gleaner*, the *Times* of London, or the Johannesburg *Star* were preceded by "dirty"? The "dirty city of New York" or the "bustling dirty southern city of Atlanta, Georgia," or "Washington, D.C., the dirty capital of the United States."

I don't think Americans would like it. They would think the "dirty" label insulting and unfair. But it is quite clearly a description nearer accurate of America's cities than Ms. Valdes-Rodriguez's or Thomas Boswell's (the neutron bomb chap) were of Havana.

What would cause otherwise competent journalists writing for preeminent American newspapers to produce such spectacular distortions? Did Ms. Valdes-Rodriguez in a schizophrenic moment actually believe herself to be covered with "black goo"? Did she rush screaming through Mr. Boswell's neutron-bombed streets to her clockless room to scrub off the goo? Or did she make a goo-impeded headlong rush to Mr. Justice's ramshackle airport to flee this godforsaken place netherward of hell? Did their various detached and objective editors accept *en toto* their claims? Black goo? Neutron bomb? Clocks? Come on. They skewed the truth and they all knew it. But what would drive a professional journalist to bend descriptions of *simple things*, physical phenomena, inanimate objects? Could they hate a government enough to violate the basic canons of their profession, to chance shredding their very credibility as journalists by inventing images that bear no relation to any objective reality? Can we believe then anything that they write? If so, which parts, now?

How much of anything American journalists write about Cuba *can* we believe? And even when a fact is accurately rendered, how emblematic is it of the larger truth or sum of constituent facts?

As I was making this record of my visit to Cuba, I received a telephone call from Martha Teichner of CBS television news. She was on her way to Cuba to do a segment for the CBS Sunday morning show. The Cuban government had been given to believe that the segment would be about Ernest Hemingway's time in Cuba.

"Mr. Robinson, this is Martha Teichner of CBS News: you remember I interviewed you in your home about South Africa many years ago."

"Yes, I remember talking with you."

"Do you still do woodworking?" She had remembered a chest, table, and other furniture pieces I had carved and built for my home.

"No, I'm afraid I haven't had a chance to do any hobby work in years."

She came then to her reason for calling. "As you know, I am going to Cuba next week to do a piece for CBS News and I understand that you visited Havana a short while ago. We're trying to talk to as many people as possible before we go."

"I'll be happy to help in any way that I can."

"We're looking into the issue of racism in Cuba."

"Racism in Cuba?" Hackles not rising, but alerted. "What would the foundation be for such a story?"

"Well, during the pope's visit to Cuba last year, the black leaders of Cuba's Santeria faith were not given a place on the pope's schedule."

"Well?" I'm lost here.

"Well, we have been told that blacks were unhappy about that."

"That would appear to raise questions about racism in the Vatican. I don't see what that has to do with the Cuban government."

"Well, the pope was invited to Cuba by Castro and we are told that blacks feel that their treatment in this case may be a sign of things to come."

"You're telling me that the pope declines a visit with Santeria leaders and CBS sees the racism as Castro's?"

"There are reports . . ."

The hackles have risen.

"I am sure there is some measure of racism in Cuba. Castro told us as much. It's a global virus. But in my view, Cuba is much less riddled with it than the United States, or even CBS for that matter. I also believe that the Cubans are trying harder to eradicate it than the United States ever has. In addition, they've made a great deal more progress than we. It seems to me that you have no foundation for what you're trying to do to these people, but whatever it is, leave me out of it."

———————

He is connecting Cuba's racial past to its present. He is more animated than before. He tugs on a beard that is ungovernable.

"Cuba had two generations of slaves. Those who were emancipated in 1886 and another generation of slaves from Haiti and the Antilles who came to Cuba to work in the cane fields. As a boy I became familiar with the Haitian immigrants. We had, early in the century, de facto slavery in the eastern provinces. The Haitians lived in poor shacks the same way the slaves had lived before. They were paid very low salaries. They lived on little food and worked hard. Noble people. It was worse than the official slavery that ended in 1886. Emancipated slaves made a cheap labor force. I knew them, the Haitians. Many of them had worked with my father and the American companies—the United Fruit Company [Chiquita Brand] and others. As a boy I became familiar with the Haitian immigrants. You understand [things] when you mix with the workers."

His pace has quickened. In twenty minutes he has recalled a century of Cuban racial history replete with events, names, dates, and analysis. It occurs to him that he has spoken at considerable length. "I took the floor and took no questions. I didn't even ask if you were interested in what I was saying." We laugh.

I ask him about the role of race in contemporary Cuba.

He does not flinch. "We thought when we opened the schools [to everyone] that that would be enough. We were wrong." He goes on to calculate the consequences of Cuba's "two slaveries," sharing with us an admission that the long developing problem was more complicated than he had thought. "We are working harder to solve it."

He tells us of the large number of Cuban doctors serving in Africa and Caribbean students enrolled on scholarship in Cuba's colleges and at the University of Havana's medical school. When we ask about the U.S. embargo, he says that he thinks President Clinton is a good man, hamstrung by American domestic politics in any ability to ameliorate the sanctions' harsh conditions.

At 3:00 A.M. Khalea presents Castro with a gift from our delegation, a book about African-American history.

After the meeting, Randall Pinkston, an African American CBS television news correspondent who sat in on the discussion, will try to persuade CBS Evening News editors to accept a story about President Castro's positive comments on President Clinton. The editors will turn Pinkston down.

On issues of race, I was persuaded of Castro's good intention. But racism is like quicksilver pressed into a hidden sleeve, left for dead, but waiting there ever ready to exploit the smallest weakening of social will.

Shortly after I returned to Washington, I received a letter from an Afro-Cuban I had not seen in nearly twenty years. I have no license to share with you his name, but some of his thoughts impose upon us the value of vigilance:

> I suspect that what will happen in Cuba when Fidel dies is that the most important sector of the white revolutionary elite will make an alliance with the white Cuban elite in Miami and with the support of the United States government try to establish a new protectorate where blacks as usual will be marginalized. That is what happened in 1898.*
>
> The difference is that, for the first time, we have not only the majority of the population but also have a black intellectual class and the Army officers who together with others from the mayor down are black. Blacks sense the danger, blacks feel the racism, but they don't understand it.
>
> We need the support of our African American brothers and sisters, to frustrate the designs of the white Cubans in Miami and Uncle Sam, who eventually will become attractive to the white revolutionary elite in Cuba. That elite has only theoretical and philosophical differences with the Miami whites. Once Fidel dies, I fear they will unite. I hope I am wrong.

Must the future always be the past?

---

*On December 10, 1898, with the signing of the Treaty of Paris, Cuba was handed over to the United States by a defeated Spain.

7

THE COST OF IGNORING
THE RACE PROBLEM
IN AMERICA . . .

We real cool. We
Left school. We

Lurk late. We
Strike straight. We

Sing sin. We
Thin gin. We

Jazz June. We
Die soon.

—Gwendolyn Brooks

SOLVING THESE PROBLEMS, the first thing is to see them.

I mean really *see* them. That is the hard part. Mustering the will to solve them is difficult but less so. Least difficult is the business of designing the mechanics of solutions. All of us look. Few of us *see*. Or want to see, trained lovingly as we are in the more genteel, commonplace, everyday bigotries. So pain-free is our indulgence of the customary blindness, not knowing that the real problem is not unlike that of the habitual smoker who felt no pain, *saw* no problem and, of course, had not the least intention of killing himself. And dead he got to be, though it hadn't seemed to deter his sightless fellow smoke suckers. Oh, they looked at him dying but they couldn't *see* the smoke killing him or them.

The blindness is pretty much universal. We've all been acclimated to static expectation and some level of socially acceptable prejudice. Most of us, the trunk and extremities of our organic democratic society, see little if anything. A comparative few of us, the uppermost parts with power and wealth, get every chance to see more but, consciously or unconsciously, elect to blind themselves—in their own narrow shortsighted interest, of course. Or is it that we're all afraid to see, fearing that if we really were to, the unmodulated demands would be too monstrously overwhelming or, less defensibly, threatening to any number of petty personal interests.

Denial is not a reflex of logic and its comforts are fickle and temporary. Seen, unseen, the smoke eventually kills.

Let me hasten to add, I am not in the least exempt from this inability to see racial disease vectors, particularly those that are silken and passive and not easily diagnosed, even when searched for.

As a young man, I worked on Capitol Hill for three years. I walked through the Rotunda countless times. But I did not *see* it. I had looked at the frescoes and friezes that I mused on in the beginning of this book and found what I had expected to find. I deflected its insult, sustained its bruises where they would not show, and kept no conscious tabulation of its message. I died some but could not know it.

"Robert E. Lee and Stonewall Jackson are in Statuary Hall. They were the traitors to the United States and defenders of slavery, but members of the United States Congress walk under the shadow of their statues every day." This was Congressman Jesse Jackson Jr. telling me this. He could *see*.

Senator Trent Lott, the most powerful Republican in government, held a membership, paid for by an uncle, in the Council of Conservative Citizens, a white supremacist group in Mississippi. The story rippled through the press. The Senate took no notice. Not even ideological liberals like Edward Kennedy. They couldn't *see* and apparently didn't want to. *Smoke kills.*

Trent is my friend. . . . I don't have all the facts. . . . The Senate can't really get into that. . . . That's awful, but . . . we've got to work together here. . . . Trent's got to live in Mississippi, you know, he's got to deal with these people.

Earlier, in 1994, the Senate passed a resolution by a 97-to-0 vote condemning the black Muslim Khallid Abdul Muhammad for a hateful speech made to a group of college students.

Later, on April 15, 1999, a crowd of protestors led by the Reverend Al Sharpton shut down half of the Brooklyn Bridge, capping ten weeks of demonstrations following the killing of a twenty-three-year-old West African immigrant, Amadou Diallo, by four white New York City police officers. The officers had sprayed forty-one bullets into Mr. Diallo's apartment building vestibule, striking him nineteen times. Mr. Diallo was unarmed and had no police record. New York mayor Rudolph Giuliani, a Republican, declined to criticize the police department whose tactics he had historically endorsed.

As the crowd, estimated from fifteen to twenty-five thousand, gathered at Brooklyn's Cadman Plaza, jury selection proceeded next door in the trial of four different white New York City police officers accused of torturing Abner Louima, a Haitian immigrant, in a Brooklyn police station in 1997.

The demonstrations, growing larger and more multiracial, had begun to spread around the country in response to the horrific acts of police brutality.

The canvas, stood back from, had a chilling Kafkaesque quality about it. Instrumentalities of the state had been used to spectacularly kill one completely innocent and defenseless man and brutally maim another. Mayor Giuliani appeared to accept this as a reasonable price of effective law enforcement. The United States Senate, having unanimously condemned a private citizen for a *speech*, said nothing.

Smoke kills. Causes unseen.

Pinstripe denial. Inside an impervious shell. No windows. Safe. Comforts. Cash. Enviable lifestyle. No ruffles. No unpleasantness, please.

Denial not only causes those cocooned to see no evil through the opaque walls of their shells but, oftener than not, obliges the self-deluded to paint pleasing murals of faux reality upon the walls.

Stephen Hunter, a white, presumably well-educated, middle-class movie reviewer for the *Washington Post*, liked the Eddie Murphy–Martin Lawrence film *Life*, about two black men unjustly imprisoned in a Mississippi state prison for sixty years. Hunter liked this film essentially because the movie was "surprisingly free of rancor and hatred." Hunter went on to write: "Two innocent black men, railroaded into a brutal penal farm system, tormented not merely by the bulls, the heat, the savagery of the place, but also by what could have been theirs and never was? Spike Lee would turn it into a napalm strike on the body politic. John Singleton would use it as a grenade." Instead, the director Ted Demme turns the black victims' sixty-year nightmare into an "essay on endurance and dignity." Aaah, here we go: "[The black men] don't let—this is their triumph, and the movie's signal accomplishment—a monstrous system turn them into monsters."

Come out. Come out. Wherever you are. Monstrous systems *do* turn people into monsters. Every day. All the time. With unerring efficiency. But those in our society who hallucinate somewhere blithely in the upper reaches of its class remove, prefer not to know this. Oh, I think they *know* it, but whenever possible they elect not to think about it. Not to *see* it.

Hiding from themselves. Listening to themselves. Put off by

an alien's anger. Praising the art that discourages its expression. The rock seated in the soggy soil of a summer bog. Better not to lift it. Leave it be.

Power with art as its handservant. Even Shakespeare remarks the gratuitous hypocrisy of the two joined: "Use power with power and slay me not in art. . . . What need'st thou wound with cunning when thy might is more?"

Because an unanswered conscience must be stowed.

Smoke kills.

In a more generous spirit, could the problem be something less than passive meanness? Could it be some form of hereditary social myopia? Of the from-where-I-stand-the-earth-is-flat variety? This condition appears to afflict politicians disproportionately. But isn't it plain enough that the fabric of our whole society is unraveling? From pernicious social alienation. From classism. From racism. From a religious materialism with the mall as church. Do I hear Nero fiddling? Or is it the Congressional Chamber Orchestra?

Yesterday, when I ought to have been writing, I watched instead news coverage of the massacre of thirteen Columbine High School students in Littleton, Colorado, by two well-armed white fellow students who were targeting blacks and Hispanics, as well as athletes who had apparently ridiculed the killers as misfits. The incident was the worst in a wave of such school killings that were sweeping the country. West. Midwest. Rural and suburban middle-class neighborhoods. White schools. White killers. And, more often than not, white victims.

Do we understand what turns children into psychopathic killers who murder at random? What this could mean for the fate of our whole society? Ken Hamblin, a conservative black Denver radio talk-show host who for some likely inane reason never takes off his hat, suggested seriously that had the Columbine schoolteachers been armed, the scope of the bloodshed might have been limited. Merciful Christ. Talk about rearranging the deck chairs on the *Titanic*. Talk about not seeing. Would giving a gun to every single office worker in the Oklahoma City federal building have averted that disaster?

The largest segment of America's moviegoing public is between ten and fourteen years of age. The movie industry puts these children in cinema seats by feeding them what the video game arcades do: action and violence. Might the movie industry's unspoken credo of profit-above-all-else have contributed to our galloping social decline? More broadly, could the quarter-century-old national climate of look-out-for-yourself-only politics that spawned Mr. Hamblin and kindred radio spirits like Oliver North, Rush Limbaugh, and G. Gordon Liddy (who once suggested publicly how President Clinton might be *eliminated*) have contributed to this headlong alienation of one American from another, irrespective of race?

How could President Clinton and members of Congress not see that this lethal social virus that is riddling our youth and stealing our future might be at least as threatening to our national interests and warrant at least as much attention and resources as Kosovo? It's as if they all jumped out the skyscraper window with the optimist in the joke who was heard to have said as he plunged past the twentieth floor, "So far, so good."

Or could it be that our national leaders really believe that the bow in which they and their wealthy contributors ride can be saved as the stern sinks?

I am anything but an isolationist. I have spent my entire career working on foreign policy matters. It is precisely because of this experience that I am convinced that the real threat to the well-being of American society is internal, not external.

I have a dear friend who until recently worked for a powerful member of Congress. My friend recalled for me a conversation between him and his boss that had gone roughly like this:

"Mr. So-and-so would like to meet with you."

"How much money does Mr. So-and-so give me?"

"He doesn't give you anything but he knows a lot about X, Y, and Z social policies."

"Does he control or influence votes in my district?"

"No, he doesn't, but . . ."

"Then why should I see him?"

Private money plays a disproportionately large role in the making of American public policy. Those who have it can come alone to Congress and get attention. Those who don't have it must either arrive in large numbers or be possessed of celebrity to get any attention at all. This is simply the way things are in modern American politics. Political office is expensive to reach and almost as expensive to retain. The money has to come from those who expect a return on their investment. The generous contributor may clothe his or her private objectives in the language of public policy, but both retainer and retained know full well how skewed by money's promise the discourse will become.

Money gives us home-use guns and the fear that whets our appetite to buy them. Money gives us the toys of military mass destruction that must be tested in battle to sustain markets for them at home and abroad. Money gives us nicotine to destroy our health and stimulate us dupes plus the industries of tobacco and health maintenance. Chiquita Brand money not only gives us the destroyed banana-dependent economies of St. Lucia,

St. Vincent, Dominica, and Grenada but indeed, gives us a destabilized Caribbean. NAFTA money gives us bad news for everyone's interests but money's. Money—big money, genuflected-to money, salivated-for money—gives us almost invariably bad social policy. For money, only and always, takes care of money.

In a 1995 film *The Basketball Diaries*, Leonardo DiCaprio, dressed in black like the Columbine High School killers, blows the class away. *Splat.* Boys. Girls. Chairs. Books. Papers. *Swoosh.* Bodies lifted. Flying into walls, blackboards. Blood gushing, spurting. Screams of anguish, fear. DiCaprio's face a mask of cool pleasure.

Many people played a role in making the film: the actors, the director, the assistant directors, the producer, the executive producer, the studio bosses. Might any of these presumably intelligent people have believed that such a film could have a salutary effect on the country's growing population of emotionally unstable adolescent boys? Did they contemplate the impact of DiCaprio's massacre on this deeply alienated band of young men who sport swastikas, take bomb-making courses on the Internet, and fantasize of wreaking indiscriminate carnage? Did they visualize them drawing lifelike blood in the video game arcades? Did they give a moment's thought to whether the studio decision to make the film was socially responsible?

Hardly. Their decisions were driven by money and money alone.

For money has become our real god, our overarching value. It is our ethic, our totem, our consuming ambition, our foremost measure of success. Its backside shadow obscures the most unsavory of means employed to accomplish its concentration in the hands of its priests. Its appetites trivialize the borders of good taste and sovereign nations.

How lonely, how foolish seeming, how futile even, it has become in our country to strive under any star but money's. There is no sweet above it, no potion more poisonous to the basic notion of one-person-one-equal-vote democracy.

Small wonder our national spirit is husk empty. We have more information but less knowledge. More communication but less community. More goods but less goodwill. More of virtually everything save that which the human spirit requires. So distracted have we become sating this new *need* or that material appetite, we hardly noticed the departure of happiness.

I talked, in the early spring of 1999, to a man who sat beside me on a flight to Detroit. That in itself was unusual, as I almost never utter a word to those I fly beside, sometimes for hours on end. Whites make up the largest part of airline passenger manifests and I never initiate discussions with white strangers out of a kind of psychic protectionism. If there is to be an exchange, they will initiate it. Usually there is silence. In this case the man beside me, who was white and on the pension side of sixty, wanted to talk about a storm that had knocked out the electricity in his Virginia suburb for three days. He had about him the quiet cheer of a well-married successful man who was comfortable with himself. "I've been married to my wife for thirty-five years," he told me, "but I didn't realize until we lost our power that we had stopped talking to each other a long time ago. Strange as it may sound, we talked to each other over the last three days more than I can remember for a very long time."

Like the thirty-year ringing in my right ear, I'll hear it if it ever stops. Few of us can see the miasma of problems that trouble our spirits. And even if we could see the noxious vapor, we'd be hard put to know what to do.

Fifteen people lay dead in Columbine High School, and days afterward President Clinton was confronted by Jonelle Mitchell, a high school student in Alexandria, Virginia, with this: "I really don't feel safe anymore. When is the government, when are you, going to do something for the other students out there?"

The president was stumped. "The federal government doesn't run this high school. You know, you have a local school board, and most of the money comes from the state." He went on to refer to the "big hunting culture" in America and described how his efforts at gun control had met with opposition.

This was all that the world's most powerful man could find to say to young Americans feeling increasingly like frightened ants. I mention all of this here because it bears on our nation's racial problems. *Seeing* that we have a problem is one thing and difficult enough. Finding the political will to confront our problems is something else again.

The growing problem of student school-building killings cuts directly to the heart of white middle-class suburban America. But to it, the president responds with an abject absence of initiative, citing the forces arrayed against him and us. The gun lobby. Organized interests. Money.

Democracy neutered. Checkmate.

Now, it would seem to go without saying that, if our political leaders show little inclination or capacity to solve a problem that the majority of white Americans want desperately to solve, one cannot realistically be very optimistic about the chances that the same leaders would confront forcefully racial problems that they have not yet even discomforted themselves to see.

Trent's got to live in Mississippi, you know, he's got to deal with these people.

Let me summarize bluntly what you may feel has been implied here *ad nauseam*: Without fundamental campaign finance reform, almost no social restructuring is possible in our country on virtually any issue of consequence, from gun control to health care. Politicians will no more act against the interests of their funders than I will act against the interests of mine. It is human nature. Self-preservation comes first for all, save a handful of true democrats like Senator Russell Feingold who risked his political career by refusing PAC money for his 1998 reelection bid.

Though it clearly isn't what James Madison had in mind, wealthy interests have bigger votes than the rest of us have. With that as a proviso of sorts, I will continue with my thought on what needs to be done to solve our racial problems. Inasmuch as I am not at all optimistic about being heeded in the near term, I will make my case unreservedly.

———

Our whole society must first be brought to a consensus that it *wants* to close the socioeconomic gap between the races. It must accept that the gap derives from the social depredations of slavery. Once and for all, America must face its past, open itself to a fair telling of all of its peoples' histories, and accept full responsibility for the hardships it has occasioned for so many. It must come to grips with the increasingly indisputable reality that this is *not* a white nation. Therefore it must dramatically reconfigure its symbolized picture of itself, to itself. Its national parks, museums, monuments, statues, artworks must be recast in a way to include all Americans—Native Americans,

Hispanic Americans, Asian Americans, African Americans as well as European Americans. White people do not *own* the idea of America, and should they continue to deny others a place in the idea's iconograph, those others, who fifty years from now will form the majority of America's citizens, will be inspired to punish them for it.

The tired swayback draft horse wearing blinders focused on the dangling carrot it could not reach. "Look ahead," it was told. "Look ahead," called the driver, as if the cause of the old horse's dilemma could ever be found in that direction.

—Anonymous

A monstrous joke was what it was. Really. Its telling began God knows how long ago. Its punch line never came. Blacks did not know the punch line although many shared in telling the joke, even while not knowing whom the joke was on. Whites didn't appear to need the punch line to laugh as the joke was being told, especially when it was being told by blacks. Something about blacks telling the joke made it even funnier to whites. This was particularly the case with well-educated, well-heeled whites of some social lineage. They looked affirmingly at each other in a way suggesting that they alone knew both the origin and the butt of the joke. Poor whites did not know who the butt of the joke was, but only that it was not them. Blacks, in the main, knew neither the origin nor the butt of the joke. They only knew that for some reason, the joke had been known for however many years as the "look ahead" joke.

Hold what you got, the saying went. And if you got nothing, hold that too. Try to think equably of your fix as preordained. The past is past. Look ahead. What past? Oops. Sorry I mentioned it.

But memory was an essential ingredient for social progress and blacks had none. Only memory would tip them off that their poverty was not fixed in nature as a condition that was meant to be. Not what had always been. Not normal. The beauty of their cage was that its constraints were not visible to the eye as were the hills that corralled the poor white hillbillies of Appalachia. Blacks walked around with their cages inside them. Each spindly little bar of the cage denoted something they didn't know but needed to know about themselves. They'd been controlled easily enough being shown things they didn't *need* to know about other people—well, mostly white people. Most blacks had come to tolerate their restricted menu of information, if not like it. Some, like the great black historian Carter G. Woodson, however, demanded that black history be made accessible to the American public. For their trouble, they got a week, later expanded to a month, dedicated to Woodson's proposition. But Africa's story before the Atlantic slave trade, which had been held intergenerationally in the memories of blacks, was inexorably misting away.

It was not always so, not even in our century. Carter G. Woodson's *The Negro in Our History* came out in 1922, his *African Heroes and Heroines* in 1939; Drusilla Dunjee Houston's *Wonderful Ethiopians of the Ancient Cushite Empire* in 1926. These historians disseminated information about Africa in magazines and newspapers before their books came out. Also,

more than a few eighteenth- and nineteenth-century black narratives speak of African glories, and reveal that many Africans
in America knew whence they came. Many black leaders of
the nineteenth century, notably Martin Delaney and Henry
Highland Garnet, knew (proudly) what tribes they came from.
Remember too that, early on, many black organizations recognized Africa: the New York African Free Schools, the Free
African Society, the African Methodist Episcopal Church. And
in the WPA interviews with ex-slaves we find that more of us
knew more about our past at that point than we were generally
given credit for.

But all that had faded by our time. The "story of the ancient
Egyptians" had been told in books and on the screen, but not
before the Egyptians had been boiled from black to white and
uncoupled from the rest of Africa. White folk had no shame
about it. I think I remember that there was even a line in the
"look ahead" joke about the genius of the *white* Egyptians. Of
course they kept away entirely from telling us anything about
the great empires of Africa's antiquity: Songhay, Ghana, Ife,
Kush, Monomatapa. Nothing in general about Ethiopia's great
ancient civilizations that spurred Egypt's rise. When Charlton
Heston played Moses in the epic film *The Ten Commandments*,
they must have confined his Ethiopian wife, Zipporah, to her
tent. Either that or boiled her white as they had the Egyptians.
We all know what Ethiopians look like and had one been cast
in the film as Moses' wife, I'd have remembered it—vividly.

Shameless perhaps, but here we blacks are, in the hundreds
of millions the world over, caged by post-slavers in stunted,
half-told, unfavorable pictures of what we were and are and can
be. Too many of us too broken, scarred, soul-weary to engage

in the full truth and glories of ourselves in the Africa way-back as well as in our American experience.

On this score, the Haitian experience stands in poignant contrast to ours and indeed most diasporan black societies. Partly because Haiti was such a grisly French killing field for slaves who were replaced from Africa with new slaves up until the Haitian slave revolt began in 1791, Haitian culture has retained more of its Africanness than black American culture has been able to. In Haitian culture, the religion Vodun promises the faithful that after death they will return to Guinée, or Africa. And almost two hundred years after the last African slave was brought to that country, Haitian paintings (of which there is a glorious abundance) are filled with tigers, lions, giraffes, and other images from a place long ago and far away—except in the Haitian heart.

8

. . . AND IN THE BLACK WORLD

Africa is having to pay a huge price once more for the historical accident that this vast and compact continent brought fabulous profits to western capitalism, first out of the trade in its people and then out of imperialist exploitation. This enrichment of one side of the world out of the exploitation of the other has left the African economy without the means to industrialise.

—Kwame Nkrumah, *Neo-Colonialism: The Last Stage of Imperialism*

AS A CONSCIOUS MEASURE, it would appear that blacks have accommodated to this long-running passive intellectual abuse all too well. Our confidence has been worn away by it like a river bed carved into rock by the assault of timeless waters. We are virtually numb now to our global position of economic bottomness. Without a better time to remember. Without a rational explanation for our decline. Without even *knowledge* of a decline. Throughout Africa and the Caribbean, in our very own countries, we occupy an economic position inferior to that of other racial groups living in our presence, more often than not as minorities. Middle Easterners do disproportionately well in the business life of Africa and the Caribbean. East Indians are similarly conspicuously successful in East Africa. Whites are usually the best off economically wherever in the world they find themselves. In America, blacks have become acclimated to being generally poorer than whites. In the refuge of our subculture, we have disguised enfeebled self-images in the escapist behaviors of people who would angrily deny the massive loss of self-confidence to which we have fallen prey in the world since the beginning of the Atlantic slave trade.

Oh, God, how routinely we genuflect to *bwana* without consciously knowing how we debase ourselves. How it must amuse whites who've come to expect their rarefied status as reflexively as we have come to tolerate ours at the world's economic bottom.

Listen to language from the government of Ghana (once led by the visionary Kwame Nkrumah) in support of the African Growth and Opportunity Act (AGOA), a bill before Congress that, if enacted, will in my view turn Africa anew into a land of U.S. corporate sweatshops:

> But not just any country is going to be allowed into the AGOA club. Star pupils such as Ghana, who have adhered closely to the International Monetary Fund doctrine for reform, will receive the lion's share of the bill's benefits, while those viewed by Washington as economic, social and political laggards will be excluded. . . . Coca Cola has faith in the economy. We are getting the big names here. . . . Perhaps an even more significant pat on the back came from President Bill Clinton, when he chose to kick off his ground-breaking pan-African mission last year by touching down in Ghana.

Could one even begin to imagine such nakedly servile language flowing the other way around, that is, out of white mouths into black ears? Clearly never. Could anything other than a wholesale acceptance of our debased state explain a kowtow expressed with such unabashed enthusiasm?

C. L. R. James, the Trinidadian intellectual, seemed to anticipate this state of affairs in the 1970s when, writing *Nkrumah and the Ghana Revolution*, he said of African nations:

At present they are allowed to create glittering units of foreign-owned exploitation, a token industrialization, which only places them more tightly and firmly in the shackles of the economic domination which they denounce and woo almost in the same breath.

I will not belabor the point here. Talk of the International Monetary Fund tends to induce sleep quickly. But certainly were it not for the blindness occasioned by Africa's damaged self-confidence, Africa's leaders would know from painful historical experience that money's Western sorcerers can quickly change costumes when there's money to be made, pawns to be fleeced. The Western strategy for five hundred years has always been to exploit until understanding dawns and economic circumstances alter, or sufficient public revulsion gathers to force a retreat. Thus, slavery was caused to morph into colonialism, and colonialism into the Cold War and the Cold War into the African Growth and Opportunity Act.

Africa pays out upwards of 20 percent of its export earnings in debt service to Western creditors, making economic development a sheer impossibility. (In the late 1940s after it had nearly brought the entire world to ruin, Germany was never required to pay out in debt service more than 3.5 percent of its export earnings.) The IMF requires its African debtors to, among other things, cut their subsidies to African farmers, schools, and health caregivers. As a result, school enrollments are falling across Africa. Inoculations are down. Infectious diseases are up. (Malaria, tuberculosis, and other preventable illnesses have risen again out of control. HIV has reduced Zimbabwean life expectancy by twenty-two years, South African by nine.) Agricultural production is down, resulting in hunger and greater dependence on American food exports. Since the mid-1980s African countries have transferred three billion dollars out of Africa to the IMF alone. Overall these countries spend four times more on debt service to Western creditors than they do on health care and education for their citizens. They are even pressed by the IMF to grow export crops in order to earn the hard currency necessary to service Western debt that never grows smaller. Sub-Saharan Africa's overwhelming debt totals more than 230 billion dollars, with thirty-three of its forty-four countries designated as heavily indebted poor countries by the World Bank. Yet neither the IMF nor the United States has done anything significant to lessen Africa's debt—debt, by the way, largely incurred irresponsibly by corrupt, unelected Cold War tyrants imposed on Africa as often as not by the United States. (For perspective, it should be noted as well that the American government's tepid response to Africa's debt crisis contrasts sharply to its response to East Asia's recent crisis, where huge sums of capital were committed by both the IMF and the United States.)

The African Growth and Opportunity Act, which President Clinton touted on his 1998 tour of Africa, does not provide for debt relief, and Africa can go nowhere economically without it. In response to calls from Pope John Paul II and an international coalition of advocacy organizations seeking total debt relief for the world's poorest countries, the Clinton administration in September 1999 requested from Congress funds for modest global debt relief. The program will have a negligible impact on Africa. Nor does the legislation guarantee American foreign assistance to Africa. Essentially, the bill promises Africa a tariff-friendly market for its products *if* African countries like Ghana meet certain onerous conditions that would make them attractive to American corporate investors. Among other things, the countries would have to keep low any taxes levied against investing American corporations, leaving the countries with little tax revenues for education, food production, and health care. Next, the countries would be required to do what American law does not allow to foreigners investing here, and that is permit untrammeled American investment in all areas of their economies. (Foreigners cannot own domestic American airlines or U.S. defense-related industries. American investors, on the other hand, have expressed an interest in owning certain African road and water systems.) African countries would then be required to sell their state-owned businesses without discriminating against American buyers. (Cash-flush American investors could well end up owning much of Africa including strategic industries and thereby threaten the sovereignty of African nations.) Further, the countries would be required to adhere to the very IMF program conditions that cap social spending in essential areas like education, agriculture, and health care.

Bear with me a bit longer, for in the basics of the relationship between Africa and the West from 1700 to 1800 to 1900 to 2000 things appear to have changed less than one might expect.

The legislation would impose no labor standards on investing American businesses. This means, in sum, that their overburdened African hires could be retained for any figure and under any workplace conditions they could bring themselves to tolerate.

The bill, as you might expect, enjoys the support of virtually the entire U.S. business community. Should it become law, American businesses investing in Africa will likely profit handsomely. But what future can Africa itself expect to have when it loses much of its capacity to educate its people, feed them, provide them with basic health care? When its hard-won sovereignty is compromised?

This is the chilling new face of globalization. The Cold War is over and this is what it was about. Money. Time to harvest the spoils. The wealthy once again dictating to the weak the terms of surrender.

Of course it never goes quite like this. In fact, I've been coarse in my summary of money's behavior. It's rather more like the show that a broker selling real estate limited partnerships put on for me once when he turned up oozing shop-mush about "due diligence," smoothly producing projection upon projection to prove what great wealth for me would be in the offing once I plunked down my nonrefundable cash.

In Africa's case the spiel may be a tad different, but the substance is similar. First the countries are, in so many words, told by us what they *must* accept. And then, with a smile, why they might like it. (Even African Americans are recruited to join the business chorus. Congressman Charles Rangel, a Democrat from Harlem, has been one of the African Growth and Opportunity Act's biggest supporters.)

Hundreds of years ago slavers held forth to Africans, whose cooperation they needed, on the specious benefits of the slave trade to (at least some) Africans. Before and after the Berlin Conference of 1884–85, the Europeans who colonized Africa did so by combining raw power with unscrupulous economic deal-making. The victim, already reduced to deference by brute power, is hard put to realize he is being conned. American policy, expressed bilaterally and multilaterally through institutions such as the IMF and the World Bank, is designed to keep Africa poor enough to supply us with cheap commodities and undemanding labor, viable enough to buy our manufactured exports, and unstable enough to provide a market for our guns.

It is not enough to lay out cold the terms and conditions of the historically exploitative relationship between the U.S. and Africa. The United States is far and away the wealthiest and most powerful country in the history of the world. Its power wears all the imaginable faces: military, economic, diplomatic, technological, cultural—I could go on here for a time. Its reputation, however, for power, the dazzling knee-buckling aura of it, often seems as potent as the power itself. This near supernatural property has a stunning effect on less influential people living both inside and outside the United States. People, places, issues, traditions, histories, cultures, deities, sports, fashions, fads, fools are important because powerful members of the American Establishment say that they are. Similarly, items omitted from America's list enjoy a lesser importance—too often, sadly, even in the eyes of those for whom such omitted items form the core of their countries' national life. America is the sun whose limitless wealth draws impoverished humankind obeisantly into its orbit for warmth and validity. There they are, much of the black and brown world, bowing to an amoral money god that has deemed them irrelevant. Unrequited no matter what. Casualties of inattention and low self-esteem. Power's disembowelment. I too am a victim. Many of the others, I know.

———

In the late spring of 1999, African American members of Congress host a Salute to Bill Clinton. Virtually at the apex of its cheer—

———

A banana farmer in the tiny Caribbean nation of St. Vincent ingests insecticide and dies the writhing death of scores of failed banana farmers before him. St. Vincent, a predominantly black country, is dying. President Clinton, being toasted now by beaming black Democrats, has killed it. He has forced a decision from the World Trade Organization that, in effect, has given the market for the farmers' bananas to Chiquita Brands, the Cincinnati-based company whose president, Carl Lindner, has donated more than a million dollars to the Democratic Party.

The African American leaders say to President Clinton that he has been a reliable friend to the black community.

Before swallowing the insecticide, the banana farmer hacks his wife to death with a machete.

President Clinton, smiling broadly, tells the black leaders how important their overwhelming support has been to him and the party.

Superintendent Chiefton Noel, the assistant police commissioner of St. Vincent, looks out over the now blighted farm landscape of the Mesopotamian Valley and tells an American reporter that St. Vincent's suicide rate has risen alarmingly over the last six years. More than twenty-five hundred farmers have lost their livelihoods. Suicide has become a way out for many of them.

President Clinton, plainly buoyed by the wash of praise, smiles with the affected blush of a gifted politician. Black guests press forward to shake his hand.

Wilberforce Emmanuel, a small banana farmer with five acres whose income has dropped by more than half, says: "I have nine children and know nothing but bananas. What I am earning now is not enough to survive."

The president's aides carve a lane for his departure, but his departure is difficult, so great is the pressure from blacks whose faces are glazed in a rictus of admiration.

Shelves in the stores on the little island are nearly empty. Eighty percent of the island's goods in years past had been brought in on boats that had once taken away bananas to markets in Europe. Now the goods are gone, the farms dying, taking their farmers down with them. And along the delicate undulating necklace of banana-dependent Caribbean islands, economies fall into the abyss like emerald beads from a severed string.

"Good night, Mr. President!"

"Good night, my friends!"

American media tend to cover only the stories that fall within the warm orbit of America's sun. It is bright there, and where almost everyone wishes to be, even those who claim to speak for those who languish unnoticed in the shadows beyond. All of Africa and the Caribbean lie consigned to those shadows with their leaders periodically invited forward, blinking in the sunlight. America's poor, black and white, live there as well.

What a funny notion this business of *leadership* has become. I'd always thought it had nothing really to do with the position of the sun, its light, its orbit, its faux warmth. I'd assumed it rather had everything to do with speaking, demanding, beseeching, fighting for the just cause, no matter where popular attentions were trained at the time, no matter where the damn sun was shining. The sun, I thought, must be moved to the problems, never the leader to the sun. But what leader, once warmed, wants to go back out into the bleak chill, even to join with old friends, even for the time it takes to do leadership's real work?

Good night, St. Vincent!

In 1994 Rwandan refugees had massed across the border in Congo. The United States had contributed to their flight by turning its back on the massacre they had only just left behind. The fetid camp was overcrowded, unsanitary, and infiltrated with killers. Unlike the Rwandans, many Albanian refugees from Kosovo in 1999 had been brought to the United States and given a year to apply for permanent resident status. The Kosovars had sat in the bleachers of a retrofitted American military facility at Fort Dix, New Jersey, where they were welcomed by Hillary Rodham Clinton, the first lady of the United States. They had been given individual beds in spotless sun-washed rooms that were wired for computers. They ate Albanian food in an American cafeteria.

Just before their arrival, the Reverend Jesse Jackson Sr. had gone to Belgrade to win from the Serbian dictator, Slobodan Milosevic, the release of three young American soldiers who had been captured earlier in Kosovo. It was an admirable feat and was covered by every American and international news organization.

No American leaders of any stature, black or white, had gone to St. Vincent. A funny business, leadership.

For blacks who would accept mantles of public leadership throughout the world, there are hard lessons to be learned if their leadership is to be, first, authentic and, second, effective. The global black community badly needs implacable black voices for its interests and causes whether they are validated by American Establishment institutions or not. We as a community must be centered enough, self-confident enough to prepare our own agendas of policy concerns and then be prepared to advocate tirelessly for those above all others, no matter where the American Establishment sun is shining. For there is nothing in the entire history of American public and private sector behavior toward Africa, the Caribbean, or black America to encourage a conviction that the United States has ever had the black world's interests at heart. Our community never gets more from the U.S. than it is willing to fight for. Often less. Never more. *What* we fight for must be decided by us and only us.

In March of 1999 I went to Kingston, Jamaica, with Hazel and Khalea to give a lecture at the University of Technology. I had been invited by Pat Ramsey, a faculty member I had met a year earlier in New Orleans. Pat is a woman of positive attitude who gets things done. That evening in the school's auditorium she had assembled an audience of nearly a thousand, including students, faculty, members of Kingston's general community, members of the foreign diplomatic corps, and at least one Jamaican government minister, Anthony Hylton, state minister of foreign affairs. The school's president, Rae Davis, introduced special guests, some of whom were old friends like Glynne Manley, widow of Prime Minister Michael Manley, and others whom I knew only by reputation, as was the case with the lawyer Dudley Thompson. Thompson, in his early eighties, had remained a vital man with a sharp mind and an engaging manner. Over the years, the global human rights advocate had compiled an impressive vita: Rhodes scholar; attorney for Jomo Kenyatta, Kenya's first president; Jamaica's foreign minister at one time, and its ambassador to Nigeria at another; Queen's Counsel, which I am told is an honor accorded within the British Commonwealth only to a select few who are deemed equipped to represent the Crown.

I'd been introduced to Thompson the evening before and had been given every impression of great warmth and charm. This was not to be confused, however, with weakness, if the stories I had heard were true. On one occasion Thompson, slated to address a major conference, found himself behind a speaker who droned on interminably, consuming both his time and virtually all of Thompson's. The story goes that, upon being finally introduced, Thompson rose and said to the audience, "Ladies and gentlemen, I promise that this evening I shall not be long, for, like the previous speaker, I have nothing to say," and sat down. This quite clearly was a man who did not suffer fools gladly.

During my lecture, I had said that blacks, victimized by slavery and the *de jure* racial discrimination that followed it, merited restitution to the same degree that Japanese Americans, First Canadians, and European Jews merited being made whole following the various mistreatments that these groups had endured. Thompson engaged me during the question-and-answer portion of the program, saying that he had done considerable legal analysis in the area of reparations (which I will share with you later).

The great majority of the questions that evening, however, reflected Jamaica's preoccupation with the damage the United States was inflicting on the Caribbean's economic health. A very distinguished-looking man toward the rear of the room rose and said in a tone of incredulity, "The United States is wrecking our economies. President Clinton met with Caribbean prime ministers in Bridgetown, Barbados, and promised that the U.S. would take no action that would hurt the Caribbean countries that have been friends of America." He left it hanging there, as if the discrepancy between President Clinton's promise and subsequent actions might be explainable.

I looked at him and gave the only answer that made any sense at all. "He lied."

The audience, in an angry mood, broke into applause. Among the non-Jamaicans in the room, reactions, read from expressions legible enough on their faces, were mixed. The Russian and Italian ambassadors appeared mildly amused while refraining from joining the chorus of applause. Indeed, Italy was a member of the European Union trying to preserve, against U.S. attacks, the Caribbean's guarantee of a banana market in Europe. The Chinese ambassador's expression betrayed little one way or the other. A couple of rows back sat two Americans, United States Information Service officers, whose facial gears appeared jammed somewhere between the well-trained agency in-country smile and the anger that threatened to override it.

I pressed ahead. "American officials abroad are invariably charming, warm, informal, and impeccably polite. They prefer to be on a first-name basis with host country officials. They entertain lavishly and insinuate themselves into the confidence of your leaders." (Among the very best I'd seen practice this art had been Ambassador Bill Swing, who during Haiti's military dictatorship gave the country's pro-democracy Lavalas leaders every impression that he embraced their cause heart and soul. He worked his magic by mixing natural charm and North Carolina folksiness with a command of creole and a dash of the seminarian's unctuousness. You forgot he was a diplomat. Saw him as a friend. Forgot that the sweet, dear man sent cables back to the United States Department of State, one of them stating, quite wrongly, that the human rights atrocities charged to Haiti's military dictators were grossly exaggerated and that the pro-democracy Lavalas leaders, who saw Swing as their friend, had duped the American Congress and people.)

"You must always remember," I told the audience, "that these people carry out instructions from Washington. They represent only the interests of the United States, as those interests are conveyed to them by the State Department. No matter how charming they may appear to be, they are not your friends. They lie. They lie all the time."

Two mornings later on the flight to Miami one of the United States Information Service officials, his agency smile fixed back in place, approached me, extended a greeting, and handed me a copy of the *Observer*, a Jamaican newspaper. "I thought you'd like to see the coverage of your speech the other evening." He smiled again and was gone. Touché.

Before leaving Jamaica, I had urged government officials to assemble a delegation of at least five Caribbean prime ministers who would come within three weeks to the United States to make the case to the American government and public in defense of their banana-dependent economies. The idea was accepted. Plans were laid. The delegation would be led by Jamaican prime minister P. J. Patterson and include, among others, Prime Minister Owen Arthur of Barbados and Prime Minister Kenny Anthony of St. Lucia, whose country depended upon bananas for 80 percent of its income. I had called Congresswoman Maxine Waters from Kingston. She agreed to cohost with me a meeting at TransAfrica for the prime ministers with influential American leaders and opinion makers. A tentative date was set. Officials throughout the Caribbean learned that the trip had been set, its mission urgent.

But the trip never materialized. I don't know what happened. It simply disappeared as if it had never been planned. The last-ditch effort to stave off the loss of the Caribbean's only viable market in the world for its bananas burned away like a rainbow in the hotting sun.

I can only conjecture. Clearly President Clinton did not want five Caribbean heads of government coming to Washington and publicly asking why the United States was doing everything possible to destroy the economies of friendly regional democracies. Obviously he couldn't say that American policy had been bought with a campaign contribution. And inasmuch as he could give no other plausible explanation for an indefensible policy toward his Caribbean *friends*, he'd have done all he could to keep the prime ministers out of the United States.

Sub-rosa stuff, of course. Through diplomatic channels. Divide and dissuade. Bilateral exchanges. Smiles in place. Address as *Mr. Prime Minister* at that level, first names will do well enough for the rest. Ready? Go.

American ambassador A: "Jim, you know that project I've been moving on for your country? Well, I think I've just about got it wired. But you know that trip of the prime ministers'? The timing of that's going to throw a monkey wrench into our project. We'd recommend that you put off the trip until we nail down this other matter."

American ambassador B: "Helen, I understand that your prime minister is planning to go to the United States at the invitation of Randall Robinson. Your people may want to rethink this thing. This won't help your case with what we've been trying to do together. You know this Robinson guy is not an insider with our people. A bit of an extremist really. I'm not telling you what to do, but you want to be careful about stuff like this."

American ambassador C: "Herm, you know my president has been working on NAFTA parity for the Caribbean. He's failed thus far, but he's still plugging. Your prime minister won't be helping him if he goes to Washington with the others and publicly confronts the president. You know what I mean?"

And thus the energy for the prime ministers' proposed trip was likely drained off through a labyrinth of bilateral diplomatic suggestions and warnings. It is not easy to take on the most powerful country in the world, even in defense of your own basic interests. This is particularly the case when trying to work the policy levers in a political culture you cannot be expected to understand. Added to this, of course, is the considerable use American diplomats make of their country's aura of wealth and power.

Think of your reaction when told that the nondescript person you are looking at across the room is a billionaire. Changes things, doesn't it? It shouldn't, but it does. It is this aura of power that the U.S. often uses to bully-charm countries into submission while giving nothing in return. The banana issue is the most important issue on the agendas of the Caribbean English-speaking democracies. It is on the front page of all their newspapers. The very future of their societies turns on its outcome. But to an arrogant United States, the issues and the countries mean little more than yesterday's swatted fly.

As a rule of thumb, given the record of the U.S. in the region, when American diplomats tell Caribbean officials that something is not a good idea, chances are it *is*. Conversely, when American diplomats tell Caribbean officials that something is a wonderful idea, be wary. Were they not so impressed by America's smallest attention, African governments would know from the straightforward legislative language that the African Growth and Opportunity Act *is* a gift horse, Trojan from all evidence. Look it then in the mouth.

This tendency we all have—countries, individuals, poor people, not-so-poor people—to genuflect to impressions of wealth brings to mind a story told to me by Walter Mosley.

The tale begins with a man and a woman at a chic cocktail party in New York City. The two did not know each other, as many, if not most, who ambulate about at such chitchchatty affairs don't. They were both white, but that detail is more descriptive here than relevant. The man was in his mid-forties and was reasonably attractive. He lived and dressed well enough to disguise having to work to live and dress so well. He made good money, lived more than a length beyond it, and was nonspecifically discontented. (As my late Caribbean father-in-law, Esbon Ross, was wont to say of Americans like the man at the party, he was "suffering from happiness.")

Across the view of the man strode the woman of this tale. She was somewhat older than the man. She wore a modest dress that did little to moderate what was remembered as remarkable unsightliness. The man stared at her with much the same interest his grandfather might have taken in one of P. T. Barnum's bearded ladies. "God, who is *she?*" he asked the fellow next to him with involuntary coarseness.

"*She* is the richest woman in New York."

"Ohhh," the man's voice trailed off, the woman metamorphosing magically from larva to butterfly before his eyes.

He then followed the woman from room to room until the opportunity for an approach presented itself. He brought it all off with sufficient aplomb to land a dinner engagement with the woman at a restaurant that she frequented but he could not afford. And thereafter, over a succession of weeks and princely tabs (which he paid), he bedded her, again and again, with inspired self-abasement. By the end of the fourth week, the man had completely exhausted his financial resources. At very nearly the same illuminating moment, the woman jettisoned the strapped chap, ending what for her had been a very pleasant and profitable affair.

There is, I think, a useful lesson in this story. Those— nations, individuals, whites as a racial entity—who enjoy the privileges of disproportionate power and wealth will seldom voluntarily do more than render to the disadvantaged an *appearance* of helpfulness. It is not in their interests to school the disadvantaged on the origins of their dilemma. Nor would they ever be likely to take unforced measures that would tend to level the playing field, if you'll forgive the tired metaphor. Never, in the march of human relations, has power behaved thus. Intrinsic to advantage is the drive to maintain itself. Aah, the advantaged. Careful, now, not to deify them. For such undeserved admiration, in and of itself, is for the disadvantaged a debilitating condition.

9

===

THOUGHTS ABOUT RESTITUTION

The world itself is stolen goods. All property is theft, and those who have stolen most of it make the laws for the rest of us.

—John Updike, *Brazil*

O N JANUARY 5, 1993, Congressman John Conyers, a black Democrat from Detroit, introduced in Congress a bill to "acknowledge the fundamental injustice, cruelty, brutality, and inhumanity of slavery in the United States and the 13 American colonies between 1619 and 1865 and to establish a commission to examine the institution of slavery, subsequent *de jure* and *de facto* racial and economic discrimination against African Americans, and the impact of these forces on living African Americans, to make recommendations to the Congress on appropriate remedies, and for other purposes."

The bill, which did not ask for reparations for the descendants of slaves but merely a commission to study the effects of slavery, won from the 435-member U.S. House of Representatives only 28 cosponsors, 18 of whom were black.

The measure was referred to the House Committee on the Judiciary and from there to the House Subcommittee on Civil and Constitutional Rights. The bill has never made it out of committee.

More than twenty years ago, black activist James Foreman

interrupted the Sunday morning worship service of the largely white Riverside Church in New York City and read a *Black Manifesto* which called upon American churches and synagogues to pay $500 million as "a beginning of the reparations due us as people who have been exploited and degraded, brutalized, killed and persecuted." Foreman followed by promising to penalize poor response with disruptions of the churches' program agency operations. Though Foreman's tactics were broadly criticized in the mainstream press, the issue of reparations itself elicited almost no thoughtful response. This had been the case by then for nearly a century, during which divergent strains of black thought had offered a variety of reparations proposals. The American white community had turned a deaf ear almost uniformly.

Gunnar Myrdal, a widely respected thinker, wrote of dividing up plantations into small parcels for sale to ex-slaves on long-term installment plans. He theorized that American society's failure to secure ex-slaves with an agrarian economic base had led ultimately to an entrenched segregated society, a racial cast system. But while Myrdal had seen white landowners being compensating for their land, he never once proposed recompense of any kind for the ex-slave he saw as in need of an economic base. In fact, in his book on the subject, *An American Dilemma*, Myrdal never once uses the words: reparation, restitution, indemnity, or compensation.

In the early 1970s Boris Bittker, a Yale Law School professor, wrote a book, *The Case for Black Reparations*, which made the argument that slavery, Jim Crow, and a general climate of race-based discrimination in America had combined to do grievous social and economic injury to African Americans. He further argued that sustained government-sponsored violations had rendered distinctions between *de jure* and *de facto* segregation meaningless for all practical purposes. Damages, in his view, were indicated in the form of an allocation of resources to some program that could be crafted for black reparations. The book evoked little in the way of scholarly response or follow-up.

The slim volume was sent to me by an old friend who once worked for me at TransAfrica, Ibrahim Gassama, now a law professor at the University of Oregon. I had called Ibrahim in Eugene to talk over the legal landscape for crafting arguments for a claim upon the federal and state governments for restitution or reparations to the derivative victims of slavery and the racial abuse that followed in its wake.

"It's the strangest thing," Ibrahim had said to me. "We law professors talk about every imaginable subject, but when the issue of reparations is raised among white professors, many of whom are otherwise liberal, it is met with silence. Clearly, there is a case to be made for this as an unpaid debt. Our claim may not be enforceable in the courts because the federal government has to agree to allow itself to be sued. In fact, this will probably have to come out of the Congress as other American reparations have. Nonetheless, there is clearly a strong case to be made. But, I tell you, the mere raising of the subject produces a deathly silence, not unlike the silence that greeted the book I'm sending you."

Derrick Bell, who was teaching at Harvard Law School while I was a student there in the late 1960s, concluded his review of Bittker's book in a way that may explain the reaction Ibrahim got from his colleagues:

Short of a revolution, the likelihood that blacks today will obtain direct payments in compensation for their subjugation as slaves before the Emancipation Proclamation, and their exploitation as quasi-citizens since, is no better than it was in 1866, when Thaddeus Stevens recognized that his bright hope of "forty acres and a mule" for every freedman had vanished "like the baseless fabric of a vision."

If Bell is right that African Americans will not be compensated for the massive wrongs and social injuries inflicted upon them by their government, during and after slavery, then there is *no* chance that America can solve its racial problems—if solving these problems means, as I believe it must, closing the yawning economic gap between blacks and whites in this country. The gap was opened by the 246-year practice of slavery. It has been resolutely nurtured since in law and public behavior. It has now ossified. It is structural. Its framing beams are disguised only by the counterfeit manners of a hypocritical governing class.

For twelve years Nazi Germany inflicted horrors upon European Jews. And Germany paid. It paid Jews individually. It paid the state of Israel. For two and a half centuries, Europe and America inflicted unimaginable horrors upon Africa and its people. Europe not only paid nothing to Africa in compensation, but followed the slave trade with the remapping of Africa for further European economic exploitation. (European governments have yet even to accede to Africa's request for the return of Africa's art treasures looted along with its natural resources during the century-long colonial era.)

While President Lincoln supported a plan during the Civil War to compensate slave owners for their loss of "property," his successor, Andrew Johnson, vetoed legislation that would have provided compensation to ex-slaves.

Under the Southern Homestead Act, ex-slaves were given six months to purchase land at reasonably low rates without competition from white southerners and northern investors. But, owing to their destitution, few ex-slaves were able to take advantage of the homesteading program. The largest number that did were concentrated in Florida, numbering little more than three thousand. The soil was generally poor and unsuitable for farming purposes. In any case, the ex-slaves had no money on which to subsist for months while waiting for crops, or the scantest wherewithal to purchase the most elementary farming implements. The program failed. In sum, the United States government provided no compensation to the victims of slavery.

———————

Perhaps I should say a bit here about why the question of reparations is critical to finding a solution to our race problems.

This question—and how blacks gather to pose it—is a good measure of our psychological readiness as a community to pull ourselves abreast here at home and around the world. I say this because no outside community can be more interested in solving our problems than we. Derrick Bell suggested in his review of Bittker's book that the white power structure would never support reparations because to do so would operate against its interests. I believe Bell is right in that view. The initiative must come from blacks, broadly, widely, implacably.

But what exactly will black enthusiasm, or lack thereof, measure? There is no linear solution to any of our problems, for our problems are not merely technical in nature. By now, after 380 years of unrelenting psychological abuse, the biggest part of our problem is inside us: in how we have come to see ourselves, in our damaged capacity to validate a course for ourselves without outside approval.

> *Meanwhile, the cotton the slaves produced had become not only the United States' leading export but exceeded in value all other exports combined. After the slave trade was outlawed in 1807 approximately one million slaves were moved from the states that produced less cotton (Maryland, Virginia, the Carolinas) to those that produced more (Georgia, Alabama, Mississippi, Louisiana, Texas)—a migration almost twice as large as that from Africa to the British colonies and the United States. With the increase in cotton production, the price of slaves went up, to such an extent that by 1860 capital investment in slaves in the south—who now numbered close to four million, or one third of the population—exceeded the value of all other capital worth, including land.*
>
> Yuval Taylor, *I Was Born a Slave*

The issue here is not whether or not we can, or will, win reparations. The issue rather is whether we will fight for reparations, because we have decided for ourselves that they are our due. In 1915, into the sharp teeth of southern Jim Crow hostility, Cornelius J. Jones filed a lawsuit against the United States Department of the Treasury in an attempt to recover sixty-eight million dollars for former slaves. He argued that, through a federal tax placed on raw cotton, the federal government had benefited financially from the sale of cotton that slave labor had produced, and for which the black men, women, and children who had produced the cotton had not been paid. Jones's was a straightforward proposition. The monetary value of slaves' labor, which he estimated to be sixty-eight million dollars, had been appropriated by the United States government. A debt existed. It had to be paid to the, by then, ex-slaves or their heirs.

Where was the money?

A federal appeals court held that the United States could not be sued without its consent and dismissed the so-called Cotton Tax case. But the court never addressed Cornelius J. Jones's question about the federal government's appropriation of property—the labor of blacks who had worked the cotton fields—that had never been compensated.

Let me try to drive the point home here: through keloids of suffering, through coarse veils of damaged self-belief, lost direction, misplaced compass, shit-faced resignation, racial transmutation, black people worked long, hard, killing days, years, centuries—and they were never *paid.* The value of their labor went into others' pockets—plantation owners, northern entrepreneurs, state treasuries, the United States government.

Where was the money?

Where *is* the money?

There is a debt here.

I know of no statute of limitations either legally or morally that would extinguish it. Financial quantities are nearly as indestructible as matter. Take away here, add there, interest compounding annually, over the years, over the whole of the twentieth century.

Where is the money?

Jews have asked this question of countries and banks and corporations and collectors and any who had been discovered at the end of the slimy line holding in secret places the gold, the art, the money that was the rightful property of European Jews before the Nazi terror. Jews have demanded what was their due and received a fair measure of it.

Clearly, how blacks respond to the challenge surrounding the simple demand for restitution will say a lot more about us *and do a lot more for us* than the demand itself would suggest. We would show ourselves to be responding as any normal people would to victimization were we to assert collectively in our demands for restitution that, for 246 years and with the complicity of the United States government, hundreds of millions of black people endured unimaginable cruelties—kidnapping, sale as livestock, deaths in the millions during terror-filled sea voyages, backbreaking toil, beatings, rapes, castrations, maimings, murders. We would begin a healing of our psyches were the most public case made that whole peoples lost religions, languages, customs, histories, cultures, children, mothers, fathers. It would make us more forgiving of ourselves, more self-approving, more self-understanding to see, *really see*, that on three continents and a string of islands, survivors had little choice but to piece together whole new cultures from the rubble shards of what theirs had once been. And they were never made whole. And never compensated. Not one red cent.

Left behind to gasp for self-regard in the vicious psychological wake of slavery are history's orphans played by the brave black shells of their ancient forebears, people so badly damaged that they cannot *see* the damage, or how their government may have been partly, if not largely, responsible for the disabling injury that by now has come to seem normal and unattributable.

Until America's white ruling class accepts the fact that the book never closes on massive unredressed social wrongs, America can have no future as one people. Questions must be raised, to American private, as well as, public institutions. Which American families and institutions, for instance, were endowed in perpetuity by the commerce of slavery? And how do we square things with slavery's modern victims from whom all natural endowments were stolen? What is a fair measure of restitution for this, the most important of all American human rights abuses?

> The founders of Brown University, Nicholas and Joseph Brown, got their wealth by manufacturing and selling slave ships and investing in the slave trade.
> The Black Holocaust for Beginners, S. E. Anderson

If one leaves aside the question of punitive damages to do a rough reckoning of what might be fair in basic compensation, we might look first at the status of today's black male.

For purposes of illustration, let us picture one representative individual whose dead-end crisis in contemporary America symbolizes the plight of millions. At various times in his life he will likely be in jail or unemployed or badly educated or sick from a curable ailment or dead from violence.

What happened to him? From what did he emerge?

His great-great-grandfather was born a slave and died a slave. Great-great-grandfather's labors enriched not only his white southern owner but also shipbuilders, sailors, ropemakers, caulkers, and countless other northern businesses that serviced and benefited from the cotton trade built upon slavery. Great-great-grandfather had only briefly known his mother and father before being sold off from them to a plantation miles away. He had no idea where in Africa his people had originally come from, what language they had spoken or customs they had practiced. Although certain Africanisms—falsetto singing, the ring shout, and words like *yam*—had survived, he did not know that their origins were African.

He was of course compulsorily illiterate. His days were trials of backbreaking work and physical abuse with no promise of relief. He had no past and no future. He scratched along only because some biological instinct impelled him to survive.

His son, today's black male's great-grandfather, was also born into slavery and, like his father, wrenched so early from his parents that he could scarcely remember them. At the end of the Civil War, he was nineteen years old. While he was pleased to no longer be a slave, he was uncertain that the new status would yield anything in real terms that was very much different from the life (if you could call it that) that he had been living. He too was illiterate and completely without skills.

He was one of four million former slaves wandering rootlessly around in the defeated South. He trusted no whites, whether from the North or South. He had heard during the war that even President Lincoln had been urging blacks upon emancipation to leave the United States en masse for colonies that would be set up in Haiti and Liberia. In fact, Lincoln had invited a group of free blacks to the White House in August 1862 and told them: "Your race suffers greatly, many of them, by living among us, while ours suffer from your presence. In a word we suffer on each side. If this is admitted, it affords a reason why we should be separated."

Today's black male's great-grandfather knew nothing of Haiti or Liberia, although he had a good idea why Lincoln wanted to ship blacks to such places. By 1866 his life had remained a trial of instability and rootlessness. He had no money and little more than pickup work. He and other blacks in the South were faced as well with new laws that were not unlike the antebellum Slave Codes. The new measures were called Black Codes and, as John Hope Franklin noted in *From Slavery to Freedom*, they all but guaranteed that

> the control of blacks by white employers was about as great as that which slaveholders had exercised. Blacks who quit their job could be arrested and imprisoned for breach of contract. They were not allowed to testify in court except in cases involving members of their own race. Numerous fines were imposed for seditious speeches, insulting gestures or acts, absence from work, violating curfew, and the possession of firearms. There was, of course, no enfranchisement of blacks and no indication that in the future they could look forward to full citizenship and participation in a democracy.

Although some blacks received land in the South under the Southern Homestead Act of 1866, the impression that every ex-slave would receive "forty acres and a mule" as a gift of the government never became a reality. Great-grandfather, like the vast majority of the four million former slaves, received nothing and died penniless in 1902—but not before producing a son who was born in 1890 and later became the first of his line to learn to read.

Two decades into the new century, having inherited nothing in the way of bootstraps with which to hoist himself, and faced with unremitting racial discrimination, Grandfather became a sharecropper on land leased from whites whose grandparents had owned at least one of his forebears. The year was 1925 and neither Grandfather nor his wife was allowed to vote. His son would join him in the cotton fields under the broiling sun of the early 1930s. They worked twelve hours or more a day and barely eked out a living. Grandfather had managed to finish the fifth grade before leaving school to work full time. Inasmuch as he talked like the people he knew, and like his parents and their parents before them, his syntax and pronunciation bore the mark of the unlettered. Grandfather wanted badly that his son's life not mirror his, but was failing depressingly in producing for the boy any better opportunity than that with which he himself had been presented. Not only had he no money, but he survived against the punishing strictures of southern segregation that allowed for blacks the barest leavings in education, wages, and political freedom. He was trapped and afraid to raise his voice against a system that in many respects resembled slavery, now a mere seventy years gone.

Grandfather drank and expressed his rage in beatings administered to his wife and his son. In the early 1940s Grandfather disappeared into a deep depression and never seemed the same again.

Grandfather's son, the father of today's black male, periodically attended segregated schools, first in a rural area near the family's leased cotton patch and later in a medium-sized segregated southern city. He learned to read passably but never finished high school. He was not stigmatized for this particular failure because the failure was not exceptional in the only world that he had ever known.

Ingrained low expectation, when consciously faced, invites impenetrable gloom. Thus, Father did not dwell on the meagerness of his life chances. Any penchant he may have had for introspection, like his father before him, he drowned in corn spirits on Friday nights. He was a middle-aged laborer and had never been on first-name terms with anyone who was not a laborer like himself. He worked for whites and, as far as he could tell, everyone in his family before him had. Whites had, to him, the best of everything—houses, cars, schools, movie theaters, neighborhoods. Black neighborhoods he could tell from simply looking at them, even before he saw the people. And it was not just that the neighborhoods were poor. No, he had sub-consciously likened something inside himself, a jagged rent in his ageless black soul, to the sagging wooden tenement porches laden with old household objects—ladders, empty flowerpots, wagons—that rested on them, often wrong side up, for months at a time. The neighborhoods, lacking sidewalks, streetlights, and sewage systems, had, like Father and other blacks, preserved themselves by not caring. Hunkered down. Gone inside them-selves, turning blank, sullen faces to the outside world.

The world hadn't bothered to notice.

Father died of heart disease at the age of forty-five just before the Voting Rights Act was passed in 1965. Like his an-cestors who had lived and died in slavery in centuries before, he was never allowed to cast a vote in his life. Little else distin-guished his life from theirs, save a subsistence wage, the free-dom to walk around in certain public areas, and the ability to read a newspaper, albeit slowly.

Parallel lines never touch, no matter how far in time and space they extend.

They had been declared free—four million of them. Some had simply walked off plantations during the war in search of Union forces. Others had become brazenly outspoken to their white masters toward the war's conclusion. Some had remained loyal to their masters to the end. Abandoned, penniless and unskilled, to the mercies of a humiliated and hostile South, mil-lions of men, women, and children trudged into the false free-dom of the Jim Crow South with virtually nothing in the way of recompense, preparation, or even national apology.

It is from this condition that today's black male emerged.

His social crisis is so alarming that the United States

Commission on Civil Rights by the spring of 1999 had made it the subject of an unusual two-day conference. "This is a very real and serious and difficult issue," said Mary Frances Berry, chair of the commission. "This crisis has broad implications for the future of the race."

The black male is far more likely than his white counterpart to be in prison, to be murdered, to have no job, to fail in school, to become seriously ill. His life will be shorter by seven years, his chances of finishing high school smaller—74 percent as opposed to 86 percent for his white counterpart. Exacerbating an already crushing legacy of slavery-based social disabilities, he faces fresh discrimination daily in modern America. In the courts of ten states and the District of Columbia, he is ten times more likely to be imprisoned than his white male counterpart for the same offense. If convicted on a drug charge, he will likely serve a year more in prison than his white male counterpart will for the same charge. While he and his fellow black males constitute 15 percent of the nation's drug users, they make up 33 percent of those arrested for drug use and 57 percent of those convicted. And then they die sooner, and at higher rates of chronic illnesses like AIDS, hypertension, diabetes, cancer, stroke, and Father's killer, heart disease.

Saddest of all, they have no clear understanding of why such debilitating fates have befallen them. There were no clues in their public school education. No guideposts in the popular culture. Theirs was the "now" culture. They felt no impulse to look behind for causes.

———

Q: What were the five greatest human rights tragedies that occurred in the world over the last five hundred years?

———

Pose this question to Europeans, Africans, and Americans, and I would guess that you would get dramatically divergent answers.

My guess is that both the Americans and the Europeans would place the Jewish holocaust and Pol Pot's extermination of better than a million Cambodians at the top of their list. Perhaps the Europeans would add the Turkish genocide against Armenians. Europe and America would then agree that Stalin's massive purges would qualify him for third, fourth, or fifth place on the list. The Europeans would omit the destruction of Native Americans, in an oversight. The Americans would omit the Native Americans as well, but more for reasons of out-of-sight than oversight. Perhaps one or both would assign fifth place to the 1994 Hutu massacre of Tutsis in Rwanda. No one outside of Africa would remember that from 1890 to 1910 the Belgian King Leopold II (who was viewed at the time in Europe and America as a "philanthropic" monarch) genocidally plundered the Congo, killing as many as ten million people.

All of these were unspeakably brutal human rights crimes that occurred over periods ranging from a few weeks to the span of an average lifetime. But in each of these cases, the cultures of those who were killed and persecuted survived the killing spasms. Inasmuch as large numbers, or even remnants of these groups, weathered the savageries with their cultural memories intact, they were able to regenerate themselves and their societies. They rebuilt their places of worship and performed again their traditional religious rituals. They rebuilt their schools and read stories and poems from books written in their traditional languages. They rebuilt stadia, theaters, and amphitheaters in which survivors raised to the heavens in ringing voices songs so old that no one knew when they had been written or who had written them. They remembered their holidays and began to observe them again. They had been trapped on an island in a burning river and many had perished. But the fire had eventually gone out and they could see again their past and future on the river's opposite banks.

The enslavement of black people was practiced in America for 246 years. In spite of and because of its longevity, it would not be placed on the list by either the Americans or the Europeans who had played a central role in slavery's business operations. Yet the black holocaust is far and away the most heinous human rights crime visited upon any group of people in the world over the last five hundred years.

There is oddly no inconsistency here.

Like slavery, other human rights crimes have resulted in the loss of millions of lives. But only slavery, with its sadistic patience, asphyxiated memory, and smothered cultures, has hulled empty a whole race of people with inter-generational efficiency. Every artifact of the victims' past cultures, every custom, every ritual, every god, every language, every trace element of a people's whole hereditary identity, wrenched from them and ground into a sharp choking dust. It is a human rights crime without parallel in the modern world. For it produces its victims *ad infinitum*, long after the active stage of the crime has ended.

Our children have no idea who they are. How can we tell them? How can we make them understand who they were before the ocean became a furnace incinerating every pedestal from which the ancient black muses had offered inspiration? What can we say to the black man on death row? The black mother alone, bitter, overburdened, and spent? Who tells them that their fate washed ashore at Jamestown with twenty slaves in 1619?

But Old Massa now, he knows what to say. Like a sexually abusing father with darting snake eyes and liquid lips he whispers—

I know this has hurt and I won't do it again, but don't you tell anybody.

Then on the eve of emancipation, in a wet wheedling voice, Old Massa tells the fucked-up 246-year-old spirit-dead victims with posthypnotic hopefulness—

Now y'all just forget about everything. Gwan now. Gwan.

Go where? Do what? With what? Where is my mother? My father? And theirs? And theirs? I can hear my own voice now loud in my ears.

America has covered itself with a heavy wet material that soaks up annoying complaints like mine. It listens to nothing it does not want to hear and wraps its unread citizens, white and black, in the airless garment of circumambient denial, swathing it all in a lace of fine, sweet lies that further blur everyone's understanding of "why black people are like they are."

America's is a mentality of pictorial information and physical description placed within comprehensible frames of time. We understand tragedy when buildings fall and masses of people die in cataclysmic events. We don't understand tragedy that cannot be quantified arithmetically, requiring more than a gnat's attention span.

> *The Negro is an American. We know nothing of Africa.*
> —Martin Luther King Jr.

Culture is the matrix on which the fragile human animal draws to remain socially healthy. As fish need the sea, culture, with its timeless reassurance and its seeming immortality, offsets for the frail human spirit the brevity, the careless accidentalness of life. An individual human life is easy to extinguish. Culture is leaned upon as eternal. It flows large and old around its children. And it is very hard to kill. Its murder must be undertaken over hundreds of years and countless generations. Pains must be taken to snuff out every traditional practice, every alien word, every heaven-sent ritual, every pride, every connection of the soul, gone behind and reaching ahead. The carriers of the doomed culture must be ridiculed and debased and humiliated. This must be done to their mothers and their fathers, their children, their children's children and their children after them. And there will come a time of mortal injury to all of their souls, and their culture will breathe no more. But they will not mourn its passing, for they will by then have forgotten that which they might have mourned.

On April 27, 1993, under the auspices of the Organization of African Unity (a body comprised of African governments), the first pan-African conference on the subject of reparations was convened in Abuja, Nigeria. Among the hundreds who attended from thirty countries and four continents were Abdou Diouf, chairman of the OAU and president of Senegal, and Salim Salim, OAU's secretary general. My friend Dudley Thompson, the Jamaican human rights lawyer, served as rapporteur for the three-day conference. The delegation at the end of their deliberations drafted a declaration that was later unanimously adopted by Africa's heads of state at a summit meeting.

I should like to quote for you parts of that declaration, for it accomplishes at least two important purposes. First, it makes known the victim's (in other words, Africa's) very public witness, which has been long suppressed. Second, it introduces what I believe to be a just and legitimate claim against the United States and the countries of western Europe for restitution:

Recalling the establishment by the Organization of African Unity of a machinery for appraising the issue of reparations in relation to the damage done to Africa and to the Diaspora by enslavement, colonialism and neo-colonialism; convinced that the issue of reparations is an important question requiring the united action of Africa and its Diaspora and worthy of the active support of the rest of the international community;

Fully persuaded that the damage sustained by the African peoples is not a theory of the past but is painfully manifested from Harare to Harlem and in the damaged economies of Africa and the black world from Guinea to Guyana, from Somalia to Surinam;

Aware of historic precedents in reparations varying from German payments of restitution to the Jews, to the question of compensating Japanese-Americans for the injustice of internment by the Roosevelt Administration in the United States during World War II;

Cognizant of the fact that compensation for injustice need not necessarily be paid entirely in capital transfer but could include service to the victims or other forms of restitution and re-adjustment of the relationship agreeable to both parties;

Emphasizing that an admission of guilt is a necessary step to reverse this situation;

Emphatically convinced that what matters is not the guilt but the responsibility of those states whose economic evolution once depended on slave labour and colonialism and whose forebears participated either in selling and buying Africans, or in owning them, or in colonizing them;

Convinced that the pursuit of reparations by the African peoples on the continent and in the Diaspora will be a learning experience in self-discovery and in uniting political and psychological experiences;

Calls upon the international community to recognize that there is a unique and unprecedented moral debt owed to the African peoples which has yet to be paid—the debt of compensation to the Africans as the most humiliated and exploited people of the last four centuries of modern history.

The declaration was ignored by American media, and I confess that I knew nothing about it until Dudley Thompson brought it to my attention after my speech in March 1999 at the University of Technology in Kingston. I cannot say that I was surprised that American media had not covered the conference. News decision-makers no doubt decided that such deliberations were unimportant, even though they had for years heaped attention upon the appeals of other groups in the world for compensation as wronged parties. As you can see, such claims were hardly unique in the world and many had been pursued successfully, resulting in billions of dollars in compensation.

After World War I the allies made successful claims against Germany, as would Jews after World War II. The Poles also laid claims against the Germans after being used by the Nazis during the Second World War as slave labor. Japanese-Americans recovered from the United States government. The Inuit recovered from the Canadian government. Aborigines recovered money and large areas of land from the Australian government. Korean women, forced into prostitution by Japan during World War II, were compensated as well.

According to Dudley Thompson, international law in this area is replete with precedents.

> Not only is there a moral debt but there is clearly established precedence in law based on the principle of unjust enrichment. In law if a party unlawfully enriches himself by wrongful acts against another, then the party so wronged is entitled to recompense. There have been some 15 cases in which the highest tribunals including the International Court at the Hague have awarded large sums as reparations based on this law.

Only in the case of black people have the claims, the claimants, the crime, the law, the precedents, the awful contemporary social consequences all been roundly ignored. The thinking must be that the case that cannot be substantively answered is best not acknowledged at all. Hence, the United States government and white society generally have opted to deal with this *debt* by forgetting that it is owed. The crime—246 years of an enterprise murderous both of a people and their culture—is so unprecedentedly massive that it would require some form of collective insanity not to see it and its living victims.

But still many, if not most, whites cannot or will not see it (a behavior that is accommodated by all too many uncomplaining blacks). This studied white blindness may be a modern variant of a sight condition that afflicted their slaveholding forebears who concocted something called *drapetomania*, the so-called mental disorder that slaveholders seriously believed caused blacks to run away to freedom. America accepts responsibility for little that goes wrong in the world, least of all the contemporary plight of black Americans. And until America can be made to do so, it is hard to see how we can progress significantly in our race relations.

On my behalf, my old friend Ibrahim called Robert Westley, a black law professor at Tulane Law School in New Orleans. Westley had been on the verge of publishing in the *Boston College Law Review* a detailed legal analysis of the case for reparations he believes the United States government owes African Americans as a group. Within a week of Ibrahim's call to Westley, I received from Westley a one-hundred-page draft of his article, "Many Billions Gone", which measured, with quantitative data compiled by respected academic social researchers, the cumulative economic consequences to African Americans of three and a half centuries of U.S. government–backed slavery, segregation, and *de jure* racial discrimination. The moral and legal merits of Westley's arguments were compelling, particularly when measured against those of claims for reparations that have been successful. One such ground-breaking claim, which had been formulated by Jewish organizations and leaders before the end of World War II, resulted in September 1952 in the Luxemburg Agreement. The claimants were two entities: the state of Israel, on behalf of the five hundred thousand Nazi war victims who had resettled in Israel, and the Conference on

Jewish Material Claims Against Germany (the Claims Conference), on behalf of victims who had settled in countries other
than Israel. The Claims Conference also represented the interests of the Jewish people as a whole who were entitled to in-
demnification for property that had been left by those who had
died without known heirs.

Westley wrote of the treaty:

Wiedergutmachung [literally, "making good again"] was unprecedented in several respects. . . . The treaty obligation by
which Israel was to receive the equivalent of one billion dollars in reparations from West Germany for crimes committed
by the Third Reich against the Jewish people reflected Chan-
cellor Konrad Adenauer's view that the German people had a
moral duty to compensate the Jewish people for their material
losses and suffering. Secondly, the sums paid not only to Israel
but also to the Claims Conference showed a genuine desire
on the part of the Germans to make Jewish victims of Nazi
persecution whole. Under Protocol No. 1 of the Luxemburg
Agreement, national legislation was passed in Germany that
sought to compensate Jews individually for deprivation of
liberty, compulsory labor and involuntary abandonment of
their homes, loss of income and professional or educational
opportunities, loss of [World War I] pensions, damage to
health, loss of property through discriminatory levies such as
the Flight Tax, damage to economic prospects, and loss of
citizenship.

Israel's prime minister, David Ben-Gurion, was to say of the
agreement:

For the first time in the history of relations between people, a
precedent has been created by which a great State, as a result

of moral pressure alone, takes it upon itself to pay compensation to the victims of the government that preceded it. For the first time in the history of a people that has been persecuted, oppressed, plundered and despoiled for hundreds of years in the countries of Europe, a persecutor and despoiler has been obliged to return part of his spoils and has even undertaken to make collective reparation as partial compensation for material losses.

The principle, set forward in the agreement and amplified by Ben-Gurion for other reparation claims that would follow, was simple. When a government kills its own people or facilitates their involuntary servitude and generalized victimization based on group membership, then that government or its successor has a moral obligation to materially compensate that group in a way that would make it whole, while recognizing that material compensation alone can never adequately compensate the victims of great human rights crimes.

Some would argue that such an obligation does not obtain in the case of the black holocaust because the wrongful action took place so long ago. Such arguments are specious at best. They can be answered in at least two ways, the second more compelling than the first.

Beginning with the question of late amends-making, in 1998 President Clinton signed into law the Sand Creek Massacre National Historic Study Site Act, which officially acknowledges an 1864 attack by seven hundred U.S. soldiers on a peaceful Cheyenne village located in the territory of Colorado. Hundreds, largely women and children, were killed. The act calls for the establishment of a federally funded Historic Site at Sand Creek. While not providing for payment to the victims'

> *In the early years of the twentieth century, it was becoming clear that the Negro would be effectively disfranchised throughout the South, that he would be firmly relegated to the lower rungs of the economic ladder, and that neither equality nor aspirations for equality in any department of life were for him.*
>
> *The public symbols and constant reminders of his inferior position were the segregation statutes, or "Jim Crow" laws. They constituted the most elaborate and formal expression of sovereign white opinion upon the subject. In bulk and detail as well as in effectiveness of enforcement the segregation codes were comparable with the black codes of the old regime, though the laxity that mitigated the harshness of the black codes was replaced by a rigidity that was more typical of the segregation code. That code lent the sanction of law to a racial ostracism that extended to churches and schools, to housing and jobs, to eating and drinking. Whether by law or by custom, that ostracism extended to virtually all forms of public transportation, to sports and recreations, to hospitals, orphanages, prisons, and asylums, and ultimately to funeral homes, morgues, and cemeteries.*
>
> —C. Vann Woodward, *The Strange Career of Jim Crow*

heirs, the apology/restitution measure, coming 134 years after the event, does counter the "it's too late" objection.

In 1994, seventy-one years after the Rosewood massacre in which white lynch mobs during a weeklong orgy of hate, killed six blacks and drove survivors into the swamps near a prosperous black community in Florida, Governor Lawton Chiles signed into law a bill (House Bill 591) that provided for the payment of $2.1 million in reparations to the descendants of the black victims at Rosewood.

Indeed, slavery itself did not end in 1865, as is commonly believed, but rather extended into the twentieth century to within a few years of the Rosewood massacre for which reparations were paid. As Yuval Taylor has pointed out in *I Was Born a Slave*:

> Although they were not called *slavery*, the post-Reconstruction Southern practices of peonage, forced convict labor, and to a lesser degree sharecropping essentially continued the institution of slavery well into the twentieth century, and were in some ways even worse. (Peonage, for example, was a complex system in which a black man would be arrested for "vagrancy," another word for unemployment, ordered to pay a fine he could not afford, and incarcerated. A plantation owner would pay his fine and "hire" him until he could afford to pay off the fine himself: The peon was then forced to work, locked up at night, and, if he ran away, chased by bloodhounds until recaptured. One important difference between peonage and slavery was that while slaves had considerable monetary value for the plantation owner, peons had almost none, and could therefore be mistreated—and even murdered—without monetary loss.)

The foregoing precedents for reparations would be less sustaining, however, had the enormous human rights crime of slavery (later practiced as peonage) not been overlapped and extended by a century of government-sponsored segregation and general racial discrimination.

What slavery had firmly established in the way of debilitating psychic pain and a lopsidedly unequal economic relationship of blacks to whites, formal organs of state and federal government would cement in law for the century that followed. Thus it should surprise no one that the wealth gap (wealth defined as the net value of assets) separating blacks from whites over the twentieth century has mushroomed beyond any ability of black earned income ever to close it. This too is the fruit of long-term structural racial discrimination, government-sponsored in many cases, acquiesced to in others.

The evidence of this discrimination is so overwhelming that one hardly knows which examples to select to illustrate the point. Westley writes in "Many Billions Gone":

> Based on discrimination in home mortgage approval rates, the projected number of credit-worthy home buyers and the median white housing appreciation rate, it is estimated that the current generation of blacks will lose about $82 billion in equity due to institutional discrimination. All things being equal, the next generation of black home owners will lose $93 billion.
>
> As the cardinal means of middle class wealth accumulation, this missed opportunity for home equity due to private and governmental racial discrimination is devastating to the black community.

Of course, benefiting intergenerationally from this weather of racism were white Americans whose assets piled up like fattening snowballs over three and a half centuries' terrain of slavery and the mean racial climate that followed it.

Indeed, until 1950 the Federal Housing Authority provided subsidies to white mortgage holders who were bound by restrictive covenants to exclude blacks from any future ownership of their real property. This device alone caused blacks to miss out on billions, in home equity wealth accumulation. Since 1950 American residential apartheid and middle-class wealth-building discrimination have been maintained through, among other means, the practice of redlining.

It follows unavoidably from this that the black middle class would be almost wholly dependent upon the gossamer filaments of salary to suspend it over rank poverty's chasm below. Consider. College-educated whites enjoy an average annual income of $38,700, a net worth of $74,922, and net financial assets of $19,823. College-educated blacks, however, earn only $29,440 annually with a net worth of $17,437 and $175 in net financial assets.

Attributing the black middle class's sickly economic condition to mortgage and other past and existing forms of racial discrimination, Westley reports:

> Blacks who hold white collar jobs have $0 net financial assets compared to their white counterparts who on average hold $11,952 in net financial assets. Black middle class status, as such figures indicate, is based almost entirely on income, not assets or wealth. Thus, the black middle class can best be described as fragile. Even blacks earning as much as $50,000 per year have on average net financial assets of only $290 compared to $6,988 for whites. Moreover black families need more wage earners per household to attain the living standards of white households of similar income. Thus whether poor or "middle class", black families live without assets, and compared to white families, black families are disproportionately dependent on the labor market to maintain status. In real life terms, this means that blacks could survive an economic crisis, such as loss of a job, for a relatively short time.

So you can see that an unbroken story line of evidence and logic drawn across time from Jamestown to Appomattox to contemporary America renders the "it's too late" response to reparations for African Americans inadequate. For blacks, the destructive moral crime that began in Jamestown in 1619 has yet to end.

Let's not mince words here. The racial economic gaps in this country have been locked open at constant intervals since the days of slavery. The gaps will not close themselves. To close them will require, as Norman Francis, president of Xavier University of Louisiana, has said, a counterforce "as strong as the force that put us in chains."

During the centuries of the Atlantic slave trade, Africa was denuded of tens of millions of its ablest people, a massive pillage from which Africa has yet to recover. During the century-long period of colonial exploitation that followed on the heels of slavery, Africa saw its theretofore viable social, political, economic, and agricultural systems destroyed by the colonizing powers of Western Europe. The magnitude of this long-running multidimensional human rights crime continues to define not only the crushing dilemmas of contemporary Africa but the here-and-now burdens borne by the scattered descendants of her sold-off issue as well. For black people, no human rights wrongdoing stands before slavery and what followed it.

Our lives—all of our lives, all races, all classes—have a regular course to them. They are habit-shaped. There is habit in the way we see ourselves, the way we see and relate to each other, as genders, as classes, as races. Habit has to it a silence, a soothing transparency. In our cluttered modern lives, charged with the burdens of the clock and the cool embrace of electronic socialization, habit relieves us of the myriad social decisions we've neither the time nor the energy to make or remake. Why throw the rice at the bridal couple? Who knows anymore? But everyone throws it. Harmless, eh? Most customs are, and habits as well. Habit does not alleviate pain. It does, however, cause us often to forget its source.

———

Well before the birth of our country, Europe and the eventual United States perpetrated a heinous wrong against the peoples of Africa—and sustained and benefited from the wrong for centuries. Europe followed the grab of Africa's people with the rape, through colonial occupation, of Africa's material resources. America followed slavery with more than a hundred combined years of legal racial segregation and legal racial discrimination of one variety or another. In 1965, after nearly 350 years of legal racial suppression, the United States enacted the *Voting Rights Act* and, virtually simultaneously, began to walk away from the social wreckage that centuries of white hegemony had wrought. The country then began to rub itself with the memory-emptying salve of contemporaneousness. (If the wrong did not *just* occur, it did not occur at all in a way that would render the living responsible.)

But when the black living suffer real and current consequences as a result of wrongs committed by a younger America, then contemporary America must be caused to shoulder responsibility for those wrongs until such wrongs have been adequately compensated and righted. The life and responsibilities of a society or nation are not circumscribed by the life spans of its mortal constituents. Social rights, wrongs, obligations, and responsibilities flow eternal.

There are many ways to begin righting America's massive wrong, some of which you must already have inferred. But let there be no doubt, it will require great resources and decades of national fortitude to resolve economic and social disparities so long in the making.

Habit is the enemy. For whites and blacks have made a habit now, beyond the long era of legal discrimination, of seeing each other (the only way they can remember seeing each other) in a certain relation of economic and social inequality.

American capitalism, which starts each child where its parents left off is not a fair system. This is particularly the case for African Americans, whose general economic starting points have been rearmost in our society because of slavery and its long racialist aftermath. American slaves for two and a half centuries saw taken from them not just their freedom but the inestimable economic value of their labor as well, which, were it a line item in today's gross national product report, would undoubtedly run into the billions of dollars. Whether the monetary obligation is legally enforceable or not, a large debt is owed by America to the descendants of America's slaves.

Here too, habit has become our enemy, for America has made an art form by now of grinding its past deeds, no matter how despicable, into mere ephemera. African Americans, unfortunately, have accommodated this habit of American amnesia all too well. It would behoove African Americans to remember that history forgets, first, those who forget themselves. To do what is necessary to accomplish anything approaching psychic and economic parity in the next half century will not only require a fundamental attitude shift in American thinking but massive amounts of money as well. Before the country in general can be made to understand, African Americans themselves must come to understand that this demand is not for charity. It is simply for what they are *owed* on a debt that is old but compellingly obvious and valid still.

Even the *making* of a well-reasoned case for restitution will do wonders for the spirit of African Americans. It will cause them at long last to understand the genesis of their dilemma by gathering, as have all other groups, all of their history—before, during, and after slavery—into one story of themselves. To hold the story fast to their breast. To make of it, over time, a sacred text. And from it, to explain themselves to themselves and to their heirs. Tall again, as they had been long, long ago.

Hazel and I went to the third-grade commencement of one of Khalea's friends last night. Imagine that. These prestigious private schools start building a child's portfolio early. We sat in folding chairs under a merciful May sun in the school's manicured courtyard. Some eighty gaily dressed nine-year-olds sat on the brick steps of a broad terrace and listened brightly to the headmistress tell them how promising their futures would likely be. At least ten of the boys and girls were black. When the students' names were called, they strode across the terrace toward the headmistress to receive their first diploma amidst flashing bulbs and whirring camcorders. A few aging alumni had grumbled privately that the school was no longer the old place they had cherished so dearly. A tad too dark it had gotten. But the headmistress, to her credit, had stood her ground, and the grumbles died before finding anything near to a broader audience. All but one of the black children came from families not unlike in their socioeconomic circumstance the other families seated there on the courtyard lawn. These black children had done uniformly well, and most had been admitted to the fourth grade in schools of their choice. The black parents were doubtless proud of their children, and proud as a group as well, even while not losing sight of their economic lack of representation of the black community as a whole. The program culminated with a formal group photograph of the class of 1999, following which the children retrieved from their various classrooms the paper products of a year's work in art, science, computer studies, and other subjects. A climate of bonhomie held parents and children together for a time on the lawn before they began to slowly make their way toward expensive cars that had been parked along the school's long, sloping driveway. As we turned finally onto the street, I saw in the distance two figures standing at a bus stop. It was a black mother and the daughter on scholarship she had just seen receive her diploma waiting to catch one of two buses they would have to ride that night before reaching home in a poor section of the city. The daughter, Khalea's friend, was bright and personable, and gave every appearance of being blessed with rich potential. But she had not done well at the school and had fallen below grade level in reading and math for many of the reasons that had explained the failure of Sarah, the twelve-year-girl I had known in Boston many years before.

What harm was done to Khalea's nine-year-old friend, and millions like her, was done long ago for profit, and with her country's complicity. Now it must properly be the country's responsibility to undo the damage and make victims like Khalea's friend whole.

But first the victims must be noticed. They must be *seen*. Early in the fall of the first grade, the mother of the little girl in this story came to the school and told her daughter's teacher that her child was having reading problems. The teacher assured the mother that the child was doing fine in reading. Unconvinced, the mother returned to the school twice in the following week to voice the same concern. She was assured on both occasions that her daughter was doing adequately well in mastering the basic reading skills. Early in the third grade, the child's final year at the school, the mother was informed that her daughter was not "cutting it" in reading and therefore would not be recommended for acceptance into the fourth grade of the school the child would normally have attended next.

The child, clutching her diploma at the bus stop beside her disappointed mother, had been cast into limbo at age nine. Of course, what happened to her happened to more than a few students at the school, white and black. In those cases, however, the parents ignored the school's assurances, sought and paid for outside help. Such options are not available to the poor, whether in public schools or private schools with vouchers or scholarship assistance. And a disproportionate segment of these child victims are black, struck down tender in a hail of figurative bullets with little idea of the direction from which the gunfire had come or why they had been selected out for special treatment.

10

TOWARD THE BLACK RENAISSANCE

Looking over the courses of study of the public schools, one finds little to show that the Negro figures in these curricula. . . . Several miseducated Negroes themselves contend that the study of the Negro by children would bring before them the race problem prematurely. . . . These misguided teachers ignore the fact that the race question is being brought before black and white children daily in their homes, in the streets, throughout the press and on the rostrum. How then, can the school ignore the duty of teaching the truth while these other agencies are playing up falsehood?

—Carter G. Woodson, *The Mis-Education of the Negro* (1933)

THE LITTLE BLACK GIRL who was Khalea's friend was told at age nine that she had failed to measure up, that she had not "cut" it. She was indisputably bright, disarmingly personable, and sun-clean of spirit, but she could not read well enough to get into the school she'd been led to believe she would one day attend. Rejected at nine.

Not knowing how to do otherwise, she no doubt blamed herself, further eroding a fragile self-esteem that had been under assault for the long heavy ages she could not know she already had borne. For in the person of a single half-soft-half-resilient child could be discerned the cumulative experience of a whole race of long-abused people.

These thoughts are about her and Sarah and Robert and Billy and the millions of children like them. They, before whom has been strung seriatim for centuries every conceivable hardship, are the future of the black race. Take no comfort from what you may see as examples of conspicuous black success. It has closed no economic gap and is statistically insignificant. It is the children of the black poor, the bulk legatees of American slavery, that we must salvage—or, in our time, we will have marked time but accomplished nothing.

It is not enough to say what needs to be done. That has been done before, brilliantly even, and gotten us little. Nonetheless, in a moment I will burden you with some of my thoughts on program recommendations. But such is not my strength. Nor is it the central point here. After all, we all pretty much know what needs to be done. Blacks know this and whites know this.

Trouble is, those who exercise control over our national public policy see no reason why they should care very much about taking steps to fix what America has done to blacks. The problem is not in preparing a black policy agenda for those who receive our votes. The Joint Center for Political Studies has done this. National black leadership summits have done this. More black groups than I can name have done this, along with gifted political thinkers like Ron Walters.

> *The politics of black people are controlled by the Democratic party and organized labor because these entities foot the bill. In fact, there is a formula: blacks supply the votes as a reliable part of the Democratic party coalition, fueled by the funding by Democrats and labor, often determining victory for Democratic candidates. Then, when blacks demand that their agenda be fulfilled, there is an impasse because they do not own their political resources and as such cannot really "demand." The end result amounts to a sophisticated form of begging.*
> —Ronald Walters, University of Maryland

We give our votes. We give our recommendations. We get little in return from those whom our votes help elect. The reason is the *politics* that connect votes to policy outcomes. In other words, we blacks don't *own* our politics, and thus have little leverage at the end of the day to enforce our policy recommendations. As long as our community must depend on the Democratic Party and other entities outside the black community to pay for voter mobilization within the black community, we will have little to no leverage to influence what gets placed on the legislative table and comes out as public policy.

In off-year national elections, it costs as little as five million dollars to run national voter education and voter mobilization efforts in the black community. Such efforts are carried out by black church, civic, and social organizations. Little of the money to fund the political work of these organizations comes from the black community, although it would seem that there is ample wherewithal to do so. Thus, we don't *own* the politics between *our* votes and *their* policy, and have, alas, little leverage over the latter. The reason? Our heads. The heads of those who could easily fund and own, in our name, our own community's politics. The heads of our children and all the rest of us. It is another price of slavery and its aftermath. We have no connecting mantra, no secular religion, no common tenets. No complete and satisfying knowledge of ourselves. With exceptions, most of us who have a little money to give have done better renovation work to our outsides than to our insides, or to our heads. As the colloquial expression goes: "it's a head thing."

I've talked enough about why this is the case. The profound consequences constitute still another particular in a long bill of them against the government of the United States and others who benefited from slavery. But this is why I have expended so much time here on the issue of reparations, for the very discussion engendered will help an embattled nine-year-old to know finally what happened to her, that she is blameless, that she has had something taken from her that has a far more than material value.

Perhaps it would help her place herself in context if she could read a letter I came upon in the wonderful book *Strong Men Keep Coming* by Tonya Bolden. The letter is dated August 7, 1865, and was written by Jourdon Anderson, once a slave in Big Spring, Tennessee, to his former owner, Colonel P. H. Anderson, who had written to the ex-slave in Dayton, Ohio, where he had resettled with his wife and children. The colonel had written to persuade Anderson to return to Big Spring and work for him as a free man:

> Sir: I got your letter, and was glad to find that you had not forgotten Jourdon, and that you wanted me to come back and live with you again, promising to do better for me than anybody else can. . . .
>
> I want to know particularly what the good chance is you propose to give me. I am doing tolerably well here. I get twenty-five dollars a month, with victuals and clothing; have a comfortable home for Mandy,—the folks call her Mrs. Anderson,—and the children—Milly Jane, and Grundy—go to school and are learning well. . . . Now if you will write and say what wages you will give me, I will be better able to decide whether it would be to my advantage to move back again.
>
> As to my freedom, which you say I can have, there is nothing to be gained on that score, as I got my freedom papers in 1864 from the Provost-Marshall-General of the Department of Nashville. Mandy says she would be afraid to go back without some proof that you were disposed to treat us justly and kindly; and we have concluded to test your sincerity by asking you to send us our wages for the time we served you.
>
> I served you faithfully for thirty-two years, and Mandy

twenty years. At twenty-five dollars a month for me, and two dollars a week for Mandy, our earnings would amount to eleven thousand six hundred and eighty dollars. Add to this the interest for the time our wages have been kept back, and deduct what you paid for our clothing, and three doctor's visits to me, and pulling a tooth for Mandy, and the balance will show what we are in justice entitled to. . . .

Please send the money by Adam's Express, in care of V. Winters, Esq., Dayton, Ohio. If you fail to pay us for our faithful labors in the past, we can have little faith in your promises in the future. We trust the good Maker has opened your eyes to the wrongs which you and your fathers have done to me and my fathers, in making us toil for you for generations without recompense. . . . Surely there will be a day of reckoning for those who defraud the laborer of his hire. . . .

Say howdy to George Carter, and thank him for taking the pistol from you when you were shooting at me.

Colonel Anderson never paid Jourdon Anderson what he owed him for his labor, nor had any of the other slaveholders (including George Washington and Thomas Jefferson) who had stolen the labor of tens of millions of blacks and, by so doing, robbed the futures of all who would descend from them. The United States government was complicit in this massive injustice of defrauding "the laborer of his hire." Of course, the injustice would not end with the lives of the colonel and Jourdon Anderson, for the colonel's heirs did not pay the debt to the heirs of Jourdon Anderson either. Thus the value of Jourdon Anderson's stolen labor was to compound itself toward the future of today through the blood lines of the white man who had owned him against all immutable notions of natural justice.

If the nine-year-old girl or Sarah or Robert or Billy is not

the great-great-great-grandchild of Jourdon Anderson, she or
he is the descendant of somebody like him. They are owed, not
just for the value of their forebears' labor, or for the humilia-
tion of performing it, but for every devastating failure since,
engendered by their government on the basis of race.

As the psychoanalyst would exhort the patient troubled
in adulthood by some unspeakable, but repressed, violation in
early life—

*If you're ever to get past this, it must be gotten out and dealt with.
Whatever awful thing was done to you must be drawn out and
exorcized.*

The chant becomes a mantra.

*You are owed. You were caused to endure terrible things. The fault
is not yours. There is nothing wrong with you. They did this to you.*

Such is the emotional value to blacks of the call for reparations, a call now expanding to a chorus that includes, among
others, the National Association for the Advancement of Colored People and the National Bar Association. Imagine all the
liberating insights rising to the surface in the tear-washed foam
of this long-suppressed national discussion on slavery, its unjust
economic penalty, and its searing social price. Billy could learn
now why there is no slavery museum on the Mall, no monument to Harriet Tubman, no memorial for Nat Turner—
indeed, why he and everyone he knows are poor. Sarah could
dream of herself as descended, just maybe, from the Queen of
Sheba, of whom, before the discussion, Sarah had heard, but
without knowing she was black and from Ethiopia.

The scale of the truth-tale balancing now, if only a little, in a
cleansing new wind, Robert could glimpse the unproud side of
European history, washing him deep, persuading him, where
no one could have witnessed his previous shame, that, when

averaged, no racial group is, or ever has been, superior or inferior to another.

> *Among the instances of [cannibalism] reported with some authority: in 1476, in Milan, the unpopular tyrant Galeazzo Maria Sforza was dismembered and eaten by a crowd; in 1572, after the St. Bartholomew's Day Massacre, Huguenot body parts were sold at auction and reportedly eaten in Paris and Lyon; in 1617 the body of Marshal d'Ancre was eaten in France. . . . Montaigne asserts in "On Cannibalism" that both Catholics and Protestants ate each other during the sixteenth-century Wars of Religion, but he does not pretend to offer proof of it, perhaps because it seemed so believable.*
>
> —Kirkpatrick Sale, *The Conquest of Paradise*

I, like the *"if I were French"* student at Howard, had never read Carter G. Woodson's *The Mis-Education of the Negro* in college. No professor I'd had at the black schools I'd attended (Norfolk State College and Virginia Union University) had put it on a syllabus. I had read the book on my own. I was stirred by Woodson's thinking but depressed as well by the still-apt fit of his views, sixty-seven years after he had written them. Progress of the "head," slavery's first casualty, seemed small. How long must a few lonely blacks whistle wisdom through the lightless centuries?

The catharsis occasioned by a full-scale reparations debate could change all that, could launch us with critical mass numbers into a surge of black self-discovery. We could wear the call as a breastplate, a coat of arms. We could disinter a buried history, connect it to another, more recent and mistold, and give it as a healing to the whole of our people, to the whole of America.

> *Upon examining the recent catalogues of the leading Negro colleges, one finds that invariably they give courses in ancient, medieval, and modern Europe, but they do not give such courses in ancient, medieval, and modern Africa. Yet Africa, according to recent discoveries, has contributed about as much to the progress of mankind as Europe has, and the early civilization of the Mediterranean world was decidedly influenced by Africa.*
> —Carter G. Woodson, *The Mis-Education of the Negro* (1933)

And then, of course, there are the billions of dollars owed to Africa and the descendants of slaves for pain and suffering, for the value of slaves' work, and for wealth lost in a postslavery environment of government-approved racial discrimination.

With respect to the question of compensation to African Americans, it has been proposed by Robert Westley, in "Many Billions Gone", that a private trust be established for the benefit of all African Americans. The trust would be funded out of the general revenues of the United States to support programs designed to accomplish "the educational and economic empowerment of the trust beneficiaries (African Americans) to be determined on the basis of need."

Professor Westley further suggests that the trust be funded for a period of no more than ten years. He does not name amounts. He is right not to do so. That should come later after an assessment can be made of what it will cost to repair the long-term social damage. By the same token, I believe that such a trust would have to be funded for at least two successive K-through-college educational generations, perhaps longer. Among other programs funded from the trust would be special K–12 schools throughout the United States with residential facilities for those black children who are found to be at risk in unhealthy family and neighborhood environments. The curricula for these schools would be rigorous, with course requirements for English, advanced mathematics, the sciences, and foreign languages. Additionally, the schools would emphasize the diverse histories and cultures of the black world. For blacks who remained in the public schools, much the same would be provided by special-purpose schools funded to supplement public-school offerings in a fashion not dissimilar to the role performed by weekend Hebrew schools for the Jewish community. All fees for these schools would be fully funded from the trust. Further, all blacks who qualified academically and were found to be in financial need would be entitled to attend college free of charge.

On the private side, a study funded by the trust would be undertaken to determine the extent to which American and foreign companies, or the existing successors to such companies, or individuals, families, and public institutions, were unjustly enriched by the uncompensated labor of slaves or by the *de jure* racial discrimination that succeeded slavery. Compensation would then be sought from those companies, institutions, and individuals—and sought with the same vigor that Undersecretary of State Stuart Eizenstat demonstrated on behalf of Jewish survivors of the Nazi holocaust, inducing sixteen German companies under pressure from the U.S. to establish a fund of 1.7 billion dollars to compensate mainly Jews used as slave laborers during the Nazi era.

Proceeds of a recovery from private interests on behalf of the descendants of black American slaves would go into the trust fund.

Now a final thought about additional programs that would be funded from the trust. The broad civil rights advocacy necessitated by a persistent climate of American racism would be generously funded, as well as the political work of black organizations seeking, as Ron Walters has suggested, to "own" the *politics* of the black community.

Lastly, I would urge the United States government to begin making amends to Africa and the Caribbean by initiating discussions that might constructively start with an American commitment toward full debt relief, fair trade terms, and significant monetary compensation.

The ideas I have broached here do not comprise anything near a comprehensive package. Nor was such my intention. What I have proposed does constitute a new starting point for a discussion with and among those who should feel some moral obligation to atone for slavery and what followed it, along with a commitment to close the social and economic gap between the races, opened and maintained by some 350 years of American racialist policies. One might reasonably ask how anyone could realistically expect the United States to take such a course when, at home, it is rolling back affirmative action programs and, abroad, providing in development assistance to poor countries but fifty cents per capita compared to the Nordic countries' sixteen dollars?

Blacks should come broadly to know that we do not approach this looming national debate as supplicants. The appeal here is not for affirmative action but, rather, for just compensation as an entitlement for the many years of heinous U.S. government-embraced wrongs and the stolen labor of our forebears. We make only the claims that other successful group complainants have made in the world. Put simply, we too are *owed*. Let us as a national society have the courage to approach the future by facing up at long last to the past.

If blacks are to have any chance for success here, we must make it clear to America that we will not allow ourselves to be ignored. I would offer in this connection a tactical suggestion: In addition to building our case on factual evidence, precedents, and serious scholarship, we would more effectively project our demands upon Washington policy makers were we to launch what I will call, a Year of Black Presence. Every black church, organization, and institution would commit to choose one day of the 130-odd days that the Congress is in session and bring on that day one thousand African Americans to walk the halls of Congress in support of compensation measures designed to close the economic and psychic gap between blacks and whites in America. The Congress, for one year, would never stop seeing our faces, never stop hearing our demands, never be relieved of our presence.

Unlike those who came to America of their own volition, African Americans are underrepresented in the councils of political power and finance. If we are to win our battles, we must fight them with the one asset that we have in abundance: our bodies.

We must do this in memory of the dark souls whose weary, broken bodies endured the unimaginable.

We must do this on behalf of our children whose thirsty spirits clutch for the keys to a future.

This is a struggle that we cannot lose, for in the very making of it we will discover, if nothing else, ourselves.

SOURCES

"Africans Prefer Whites to Blacks in SA." *New York Times*, October 19, 1998.

Anderson, S.E. *The Black Holocaust for Beginners*. New York: Writers and Readers Publishing, 1995.

Baigent, Michael and Richard Leigh. *The Temple and the Lodge*. New York: Arcade, 1989.

Baldwin, James. *Nobody Knows My Name*. New York: Dial, 1961.

Bittker, Boris. *The Case for Black Reparations*. New York: Random House, 1973.

Bohlen, Celestine. "Illusions Shattered in St. Petersburg." *New York Times*, November 29, 1998.

Bolden, Tonya. *Strong Men Keep Coming*. New York: John Wiley & Sons, 1999.

Boswell, Thomas. "The National Pastime Is Despair." *Washington Post*, March 28, 1999.

Broder, John. "Clinton Apologizes for U.S. Support of Guatemalan Rightists." *New York Times*, March 11, 1999.

Bronner, Ethan. "U. of Washington Will End Race-Conscious Admissions." *New York Times*, November 7, 1998.

Burgess, John "26 Poorest Nations Get Debt Break" *Washington Post*, September 27, 1999.

Catholic Encyclopedia. http://www.knight.org/advent.

Coates, Ta-Nehisi. "Case History: How the Effort to Build an African-American Museum on the Mall Ended Up in a Black Hole." *Washington City Paper* 18, no. 5 (February 6–12, 1998).

Davidson, Basil, *Africa in History*. New York: Collier Books, 1991.

———. *African Civilization Revisited*. Lawrenceville, N.J.: Africa World Press, Inc., 1991.

———. *The African Genius*. Boston: Little, Brown, 1969.

———. *The African Slave Trade*. Revised edition. Boston: Back Bay/Little, Brown, 1980.

———. *The Black Man's Burden*. New York: Times Books, 1992.

. *The Lost Cities of Africa*. Boston: Little, Brown, 1959.

———. *A Search for Africa*. New York: Times Books, 1994.

Fisher, Ian. "Is Lewinsky's Boswell a Flatterer? Ask These Folks." *New York Times*, November 26, 1998.

Fletcher, Michael A. " 'Crisis' of Black Males Gets High-Profile Look." *Washington Post*, April 17, 1999.

Franklin, John Hope. *From Slavery to Freedom*. New York: Knopf, 1947.

"Genghis Kahn." *National Geographic*. Vol. 190, No. 6, 1996.

Gourevitch, Philip. *We Wish to Inform You That Tomorrow We Will Be Killed with Our Families*. New York: Farrar, Straus & Giroux, 1998.

Herbert, Bob. "G.O.P. Cover Story." *New York Times*, October 11, 1998.

Herodotus. *The Histories*. New York: Penguin Classics, 1954.

Hochschild, Adam. *King Leopold's Ghost*. Boston: Houghton Mifflin, 1998.

Holmes, Steven A. "Clinton Panel on Race Urges Variety of Modest Measures." *New York Times*, September 7, 1998.

Hunter, Stephen. "Mightier Than the Pen." *Washington Post*, April 16, 1999.

James, C.L.R. *Nkrumah and the Ghana Revolution*. Chicago: Lawrence Hill, 1977.

Jefferson, Thomas. *Notes on the State of Virginia*. Chapel Hill: University of North Carolina Press, 1954.

Justice, Richard. "O's Cuba Trip Is Scored a Hit by Officials." *Washington Post*, March 30, 1999.

Kelly, I.N.D. The Oxford Dictionary of Popes. Oxford, 1986.

Kozol, Jonathan. *Savage Inequalities*. New York: Crown, 1991.

Krauss, Clifford. "The Spies Who Never Came In From the Cold War." *New York Times*, March, 7, 1999.

Lamb, Christina. "U.S. Action on Bananas a Nightmare for Islands." *Washington Times*, March 16, 1999.

Le Riverend, Julio. *Brief History of Cuba*. Havana: Instituto Cubano del Libro, 1997.

Leonard, Elmore. *Cuba Libre*. New York: Delacorte, 1998.

Mahon, Nancy. "The Problem with Private Prisons." *Washington Post*, November 1, 1998.

Manley, Michael. *The Politics of Change*. Washington, D.C.: Howard University Press, 1975.

Matthews, Marcia M. *Henry Ossawa Tanner: American Artist*. Chicago: University of Chicago Press, 1969.

Maxwell-Stuart, P. G. *Chronicle of The Popes*. New York: Thames and Hudson, 1997.

Mazrui, Ali A. *The Africans: A Triple Heritage*. Boston: Little, Brown, 1986.

Merida, Kevin. "3 Consonants and a Disavowal." *Washington Post*, March 29, 1999.

Neal, Terry M. "For Blacks, an Issue of Pressure vs. Prudence." *Washington Post*, November 23, 1998.

New Advent: Catholic Supersite. http://www.knight.org/advent/popes.

Paine, Thomas. "African Slavery in America." *Pennsylvania Journal and Weekly Advertiser*, March 8, 1775.

Pincus, Walter. "Spy Suspect Fired at Los Alamos Lab." *Washington Post*, March 9, 1999.

Poe, Richard. *Black Spark, White Fire*. Prima, 1998.

"Racial Factor Seen in Test White House Did for Drugs." *New York Times*, October 7, 1998.

Reynolds, Patrick M. *A Cartoon History of the District of Columbia*. Red Rose Studio, 1995.

Rosenbaum, David E. "U.S. Threatens Europe with 100% Tariffs." *New York Times*, November 11, 1998.

Sack, Kevin. "Blacks Stand by a President Who 'Has Been There for Us.' " *New York Times*, September 19, 1998.

Safire, William. "American Defeat." *New York Times*, March 8, 1999.

Sale, Kirkpatrick. *The Conquest of Paradise*. New York: Knopf, 1990.

Seelye, Katharine Q. "Clinton Seeks to Console Students But Falters." *New York Times*, April 23, 1999.

Slavery in America. PBS television series, October 1998.

Smith, Leef. "Tests Link Jefferson, Slave's Son." *Washington Post*, November 1, 1998.

Taylor, Yuval, ed. *I was Born A Slave* (vol. 1). Chicago: Lawrence Hill, 1999.

Thomas, Hugh. *The Slave Trade.* New York: Simon and Schuster, 1997.

Thomas, Velma M. *Lest We Forget.* New York: Crown, 1997.

United States Capitol Historical Society. *"The Apotheosis of George Washington."*

Updike, John. *Brazil.* New York: Knopf, 1994.

Valdes-Rodriguez, Alisa. "Our Man Woody in Havana." *Los Angeles Times*, April 2, 1999.

Wamba, Philippe. *Kinship.* New York: Dutton, 1999.

Weiner, Tim, and James Risen. "Decision to Strike Factory in Sudan Based on Surmise." *New York Times*, September 21, 1998.

Westley, Robert. "Many Billions Gone." *Boston College Law Review*, June 1999.

Wilgoren, Jodi. "Diallo Rally Focuses on Call for Strong Oversight of Police." *New York Times*, April 16, 1999.

Williams, Eric. *From Columbus to Castro.* New York: Vintage, 1970.

Wolfe, Thomas. *You Can't Go Home Again.* New York: Harper, 1940.

Woodson, Carter G. *The Mis-Education of the Negro.* Washington, D.C.: Associated Publishers, 1933.

X, Malcolm. *The Autobiography of Malcolm X.* New York: Grove Press, 1965.

INDEX